In the Narrow Places:
Daily Inspiration for the Three Weeks

Erica Brown

IN THE NARROW PLACES

DAILY INSPIRATION FOR THE THREE WEEKS

Maggid Books & OU Press

In the Narrow Places:
Daily Inspiration for the Three Weeks

First Edition, 2011
Maggid Books
An imprint of Koren Publishers Jerusalem Ltd.

POB 8531, New Milford, CT 06776-8531, USA
POB 4044, Jerusalem 91040, Israel

www.korenpub.com

ISBN 978 159 264 340 0, *hardcover original*

A CIP catalogue record for this title is
available from the British Library

Printed in USA

Contents

v

Acknowledgments

*I*n the *Narrow Places* was not written from a narrow place. It was written with the excellent support and thoughtfulness of Gil Student and those at OU PRESS, and Mathew Miller and his team at Koren Publishers Jerusalem. I write this with the immense support of the Jewish Federation of Greater Washington, the Wexner Foundation, the Mandel Foundation, the Covenant Foundation and Avi Chai Foundation. It was written from a place of enormous blessings; my family, my friends, my community and my colleagues have all made my life and my work exceptionally expansive. I thank God for all of these blessings. Perhaps, as a result of this expansiveness, I have not been able to capture fully the experience of loss that inspired the writing of this book. For that I take full responsibility.

This book honors the memory of dozens of family members I never met who lost their lives in a small Polish town, Zakrzewek, on October 18, 1942, when the SS gathered the 600 remaining Jews in the town and murdered them simply for being Jewish. It is, in my family narrative, what one sociologist has called "a legacy in the form of absences." It is the closest touch-point that I have for the Ḥurban, the destruction of the Temples, Jerusalem and all those who lost their lives then. May

Acknowledgments

the memory of these tragic victims be for a blessing and a signpost that persecution will lead to redemption because we will make it so.

Erica Brown
Silver Spring, MD
Adar II 5771 / March 2011

Introduction

When Memory Speaks

Of all of the milestones and Holidays that are celebrated or commemorated by the Jewish calendar, no time period is more neglected than that of the "Three Weeks." This snatch of mid-summer anxiety is virtually unknown outside of the observant Jewish community; perhaps in some far-away mental archive the term "Tisha B'Av," the ninth day of the Hebrew month of Av, registers as a Jewish fast day. The broader time period – if recognized at all – is for only the "very religious." Many other rituals, formerly regarded as limited to the domain of the intensely pious, have made their way into broader Jewish culture; even if they are not observed, they at least garner some recognition. Tisha B'Av and the Three Week period do not. Even among those who observe Tisha B'Av, many consider it an inconvenient and meaningless obligation.

Along with Yom Kippur, Tisha B'Av is the most demanding of the year's liturgy of fast days. It is the longer of the two, and possibly the harder, coming as it does during the summer months. While Yom Kippur is oriented towards both the past and the future, Tisha B'Av seems focused exclusively on the past: along with memorializing the destruction of the two Temples, it jumbles together all the tragedies of Jewish history. Yet there is an intrinsic linkage between the two days. The Day of Atonement's repentance is personally cathartic. Tisha B'Av's mourning is nationally cathartic. It allows us to grieve as a unit and then move on, strengthening our national identity by rebuilding from the ashes of memory. In *Against Identity*, Leon Wieseltier argues that "identity in bad times is not like identity in good times. The vigorous expression of identity in the face of oppression is not an exercise of narcissism, it is an exercise of heroism."[1] And yet, despite the benefits of such a communal enactment of history, such an implantation of identity and even heroism, the Jewish community at large has not embraced Tisha B'Av.

Why has this day and its surrounding rituals not been appreciated by the wider Jewish community? Perhaps the answer lies in a particular type of amnesia, a willed disregard for tragic history or the past. Rabbi Joseph B. Soloveitchik observed that American Jews do not always have sufficient sensitivity to Torah values to achieve spiritual depth.

> Human happiness does not depend on comfort. The American Jew follows a philosophy which equates religion with making Jewish life more comfortable and convenient. It enables the Jew to have more pleasure in life. This de-emphasizes Judaism's spiritual values."[2]

Comfort is the main obstruction blocking the Jewish community from contact with Tisha B'Av. Yet the selective amnesia towards the traumatic history that Tisha B'Av mourns has not influenced the pervasive impact of the Holocaust on contemporary Jewish life. Indeed, our collective memory seems to stop there: the Holocaust has replaced the history which preceded it.

Perhaps then the issue is also – *what* is remembered. The Holocaust is widely memorialized, with or without religious overtones, because of the death of much of European Jewry. Understandably, for many, the destruction of a building, even one as significant as the *Beit HaMikdash*, the Temple, could never compare. But the destruction of

1. Leon Wieseltier, *Against Identity* (New York: William Drenttel, 1996), p. 14.
2. Rabbi Aaron Rakeffet-Rothkoff, *The Rav: The World of Rabbi Joseph B. Soloveitchik*, Vol. II (Jersey City, NJ: KTAV Publishing House, 1999), p. 18.

a building is not only, or predominantly, what Tisha B'Av mourns. It mourns the loss of an aspect of our relationship with God, the loss of the God who dwells within us, of a religious center and capital city, and the destruction of all those who lived during that period.

There was a time when it was important to know the place you came from in the broadest sense, to have a master narrative of a people as a bedrock for your own values. It grounded you, and gave you direction – if you know where you come from, you arguably have a better sense of where you are going. Tisha B'Av is best observed by those who appreciate history and understand that a nation must look back if it is to look forward. Examining the vicissitudes and errors of the past helps you correct them in the future. Cicero, the renowned Roman statesman and orator, once said, "To remain ignorant of things that happened before you were born is to remain a child." There is an immaturity about individuals who have no grip on history. There is an immaturity about nations that have disregarded the past and only look at the present and to the future.

To be part of Western civilization today, however, is largely to act ahistorically. This does not mean that we despise history or repudiate it; it is enough to ignore it. American holidays are generally commemorated without a historical context; the rituals that are celebrated are neither deep nor transformational. They are surface sacraments that, in a multicultural society, no longer have the power and potency of a shared language of meaning or of nostalgia. Think only of Thanksgiving and the way that it is observed in America today, and you will see how this sad reality plays itself out on our national landscape. Turkey dinners and football games will hardly inspire a nation, much less a melting pot of people for whom turkey is not part of a national diet or football a national pastime. Memorial Day is not observed as a mourning period for the loss of soldiers; it is a day of barbeques, sales and public-pool openings. There is a shallowness about it all, the childishness that Cicero observed. American Jews are naturally enmeshed in the culture in which they live, and Americans, as members of a young country, do not have a long historical memory. Nor does the youthful American spirit, with its emphasis on moving forward, encourage its citizens to look backward with awe, respect, sadness and gratitude.

In addition, we live in a period that is enormously invested in happiness. Just type "books on happiness" into Amazon and see what you come up with (by my count, it's close to 17,000). We guard our happiness closely, and do not want to mar it with sad thoughts. We fail to view suffering as a natural part of human life – living in such relative comfort as we do, suffering always takes us by surprise, as if it were an injustice. And as it is an injustice, we look for someone to blame. Sharon Salzberg, in her book *Lovingkindness*, points out that

> we feel obliged to defend our happiness because it seems so frag-
> ile, unstable. As though our happiness needed constant protec-
> tion, we deny the very possibility of suffering; we cut ourselves
> off from facing it in ourselves and in others because we fear that
> it will undermine or destroy our good fortune.[3]

Suffering humanizes us. Ignoring suffering dehumanizes us. I don't want to ruin my good mood by looking at that homeless person, so I turn away – and with that turning, I let go of my social responsibility to him. Attunement to suffering makes us more compassionate. It also helps us appreciate where we come from and all that it took to get us to where we are. We have to remind ourselves that we don't diminish our happiness when we spend a day or a few weeks meditating on the tragedies of history from which we emerged. We become more grateful, holding on tightly to our blessed lives because we can.

To quote Cicero again: "History is the witness that testifies to the passing of time; it illumines reality, vitalizes memory, provides guidance in daily life and brings us tidings of antiquity." For Jews, these tidings of antiquity are not merely a charm one finds in an antique shop, something quaint, sentimental, and useless. Rather, history is one of the key connectors that enables us to discover a shared life together. And history is not only about that which we once celebrated together. History, in its most profound sense, is the joint language of pain that forms the crucible of peoplehood. In simple human terms, we know that when

---

3. Sharon Salzberg, *Lovingkindness: The Revolutionary Art of Happiness* (Boston: Shambhala Publications Inc., 2008), p. 12.

strangers undergo a tragedy together, they form intense and unique bonds. Something life-changing happened in the presence of another, and both parties may be transformed forever as a result. Both need each other as reminder and witness.

Tisha B'Av is precisely this reminder to us as Jews to take the time to mark difficulties, not escape from them. It is not a great sacrifice to ask people to fast once a year as a way of mourning together the persecutions, destructions and calamities of our nation. Before its renovation, inscribed above the exit of *Yad Vashem*, Israel's Holocaust museum, was a quote attributed to the Ba'al Shem Tov that communicated what loss of memory costs: "Forgetfulness leads to exile, while remembrance is the secret of redemption." Memory is our collective glue; it brings us together, united by a common narrative of the past, a master story that advances a vision of redemption for the future. But if we forget, we are no longer anchored by our deepest values and core beliefs. Memory enables us to restate our values in the presence of each other. We are at that nexus in history when we can complete the message.

Tisha B'Av also reminds us that there is a language of pain, a way to articulate suffering. The period of the Three Weeks is captured in the prose-poetry of Jeremiah, in the wailing women of Lamentations, in the protests of Job. Our summer reading is temporarily replaced by more strenuous language that offers us the linguistic tools to speak about tragedy, to plumb its depths and encircle our hearts at the same time. Each year, we encounter these texts anew. We read them into recent news broadcasts and personal distress; we marvel at the way that these ancient voices pierce our modern reality and offer a way of understanding a world that can seem confusing and disorienting.

BUT WHY IS IT SO HARD?

Even when we recognize the cognitive importance of recalling the past, we are not always capable of rising to the emotional challenge of reliving it. Instead, we often find ourselves immersed in the particularities of Jewish law, reviewing the minutiae of observance, not always as a preparation for this period but often as a *distraction*. If we lose ourselves in the questions of whether or not to listen to music on a radio, buy particular objects of clothing if they are discounted, or engage in

5

instructional swimming, we may avoid the more essential task of the season: creating genuine sorrow over the incalculable loss of our Jewish spiritual center. We measure ourselves by outward displays of mourning – the unshaven beard, the unironed clothes, the limitations on external expressions of happiness – but the heart often remains untouched. The halakhic restrictions of the period help us structure our worlds to minimize joy but they cannot force sadness; they can only minimize the conditions for happiness.

Rabbi Abraham Isaac HaKohen Kook, the first chief rabbi of Israel (then Palestine), underscored this emotional absence in our observance in a letter he wrote in 1913, referencing those who teach Torah:

> Our most talented people concentrated for the most part on the practical aspects of the Torah, and even there only on specialized subjects. This they cultivated and made it the habituated subject of education. The emotional aspect, and more than this, the philosophical, and that which is beyond it and follows it automatically, the illumination of holiness, which bears within itself the mystery of the redemption – this they abandoned altogether.[4]

If those who teach Torah cannot grasp the illumination of holiness, then what about those of us who learn from them? What chance do we have? Genuine grief comes not from deprivation, but from a place of reflection and contemplation on the nature and content of our common historical losses, and the spiritual anguish we experienced in their wake.

Sometimes the deprivations mandated by Jewish law loom so large as to block out the deeper content. The Three Weeks fall in the middle of summer, dampening the weather and the usual summer breeziness of outdoor activities and much-needed vacations. In the minds of many, the period of the Three Weeks becomes a spoiler. It makes demands at a time of year which is usually demand-free – if not in reality, then at least in perception: school is out, and workloads lighten. The adoption

4. Rabbi Abraham Isaac HaKohen Kook, letter to Rabbi Judah Leib Seltzer (1913), found in *Abraham Isaac Kook*, translated by Ben Zion Bokser (London: SPCK, 1978), p. 354.

of a strict set of guidelines in the middle of this season is often thought of – if rarely articulated – as an invasion of personal enjoyment.

A friend once remarked, "I would trade Three Weeks in the summer for five weeks in the winter," underscoring how difficult the summer season is for the expression of pain. It is hard to enforce sadness when our natural inclination is to turn our heads to the sun and feel the warmth and relief of a gorgeous summer day. Traditionally, Jews make holiday plans immediately following Tisha B'Av, as if to suggest that sadness is now officially "over and done with." We await that day after, and through that anticipation negate the importance of the time period itself.

In addition to the pull of summer laziness and freedom, the Three Weeks cut into our modern notions of hygiene and comfort. When the laws of this period were originally created, people did not bathe with the kind of regularity to which we are accustomed. If one is a product of an era where there are few expectations of personal comfort, then refraining from regular, lengthy and hot showers or from wearing clean clothing is less of a sacrifice. Indeed, it is important to recognize that people were not accustomed to being able to control the temperature in their homes, and lived without the pampering modern conveniences that protect us from experiencing the challenging and messy elements of nature. The fact that clothes go unlaundered for nine days may have once been only a slight aberration in a medieval laundry schedule. Today, it is a remarkable deviation.

Fasting is also a challenge. Along with the wearing of sackcloth, fasting is an ancient biblical behavior that was regarded as a way to curb happiness through curbing appetite. Ideally, fasting should remove us enough from our everyday lives to help us step outside ourselves and question our actions and motivations, while not proving so much of a challenge that it gets in the way of genuine repentance and contemplation. In an age of so much food consumption, however, fasting becomes much harder. When one had scant provisions and perhaps ate only one large meal a day, fasting merely demanded a slightly greater staying power than usual. Today, it can become a distraction from our best intentions.

Indeed, the prophets attest that even in biblical times, people often forgot that fasting is but a means to an end – repentance – and made it instead an end in itself. In the words of Zechariah:

> Speak to all the people of the land, and to the priests, saying,
> When you fasted…was it for Me that you really fasted? And
> when you did eat, and when you did drink, did you not eat for
> yourselves, and drink for yourselves? (Zechariah 7:5–6)

Fasting did little to change the ancient Israelites according to this prophet
and many others; it did not leave any internal marks:

> And they made their hearts an adamant stone, lest they should
> hear the Torah, and the admonition of the prophets… And so,
> when He cried, and they would not hear, the Lord of hosts said:
> So shall they cry, and I will not hear. (Zechariah 7:12–13)

Without good intentions and real transformation, fasting fails its purpose.

The day of Tisha B'Av itself is demanding – and not only because
of fasting and other physical restrictions. The liturgy of the day is obscure
and esoteric. We move from Jeremiah's eye-witness account of Jerusalem's destruction in *Eikha*, the book of Lamentations, to reams of medieval acrostics that use scholarly referencing and cross-referencing to the
Bible, Talmud and Midrash. Each *kina* (lament) poses a literary wall of
obscurity. In the aggregate, we feel overwhelmed less by sadness than
by incomprehension.

Many synagogues and individuals focus on a selection of the
laments for this very reason. This reduces the amount of material, but
not the challenge of understanding it. Quick summaries that bring sim-
plicity to the language actually diminish the authorial intent of these
kinot as literary puzzles that require intense focus and an in-depth facil-
ity with language and nuanced biblical references. One can only imagine the response of a member of the pietistic Kalonymus family, from
which many of our Tisha B'Av supplications originate, if he were sitting
in a synagogue today as his words were introduced and summarized
in a sentence or two, then recited quickly by individual congregants.
"But how could you miss the acrostic? The word-play? The reference to
Job, and to Lamentations? You jumped over the chiasms and subtleties
without pausing, even for a moment." Those who have studied even one
kina with a detailed line-by-line exegesis, will no doubt appreciate that

any thorough approach would require weeks of comprehensive study. Instead, we find synagogues littered with people on the floor, bent over their canvas shoes, with their lips moving and their eyes blankly glazed with intellectual dismay. It is the look of being lost, not of being emotionally engaged.

We wait for a *kina* that describes an event we recognize, or one that uses language familiar to us, or a tune that overcomes the difficulty of the words by joining us in the outward form of a haunting melody. One of the last *kinot*, now included by many, marks the Holocaust, and it usually induces a deeper level of involvement because it marks an event closer in time. I recall once being in a synagogue where congregants took turns leading the recitation of *kinot*. The older man who began the Holocaust *kina* suddenly stuttered on the first words and began to cry. Trying but unable to catch himself, he finally said, "Rabbi, pick someone else to read. I can't do it." The rabbi responded, "Better we should have someone read it who has less feeling? We'll wait." And we did. I have never heard this prayer more movingly read. Mostly, however, these prayers seem to present a thick fog of language that, because of our lack of understanding, blocks rather than enhances the path to reliving tragedy.

We have never experienced Jewish life with the Temple, the *Mikdash*. How then can we know what we are missing? To express this more boldly and radically, there are many very religious individuals who secretly harbor anxiety over the very possibility that a third Temple would be rebuilt. Between the notion of animal sacrifices and the denominationalism whose fissures are dividing us, we privately fear what life with a *Mikdash* would be like. We might find ourselves wondering about the smell of blood, the cost of membership and maintenance, the usher at the door ensuring that we are sufficiently pure to enter Temple precincts. Everything about it seems either a projection of current synagogue life on a bigger scale, or an anachronistic forcing of the past unrealistically onto the future.

Rabbi Moshe Feinstein discusses the emotional and intellectual challenges presented by Tisha B'Av in one of his *teshuvot*, responsum. He was asked about children and their observance of mourning, and explains why children have to observe the laws of Tisha B'Av despite its myriad cognitive challenges. He writes that while children lack the capacity to suffer a loss they have not experienced, we must understand that every year that the *Beit HaMikdash* is not rebuilt is the equivalent of a year when it has been destroyed. If such is our annual reality, then children are obliged to experience this loss again and again in order to mature into it. If the intention of the season is to pay respects to the *Beit HaMikdash*, then it is essential to understand that it was a central feature of our past and without it, many mitzvot cannot be observed today. Tisha B'Av then becomes an important educational opportunity.[5] What is true for children is all the more true for adults who should have the imaginative capacity to recreate a lost spiritual universe.

Tisha B'Av asks something difficult of us: can we mourn that which we have never personally experienced? The Talmud illustrates this imaginative capacity with a story about Rabbi Yehudah bar Ilai, a second-century *tanna* from the Galilee.

> Rabbi Yehuda said in the name of Rav: This was the practice of Rabbi Yehuda son of Ilai. On Tisha B'Av eve they would bring him bread dipped in salt and he would sit between the oven and the furnace and eat. He drank a flask of water along with his bread and his appearance was that of one whose deceased relative lies before him. (*Ta'anit* 30a)

Rabbi Yehuda personalized his grief and made it real. He sat in a lowly place where he could see flames, and he wore the garments of mourning and ate the food of mourners and thus, became a mourner.

Even God, in the Talmud, has the capacity to embody the grief of humans as an empathetic response:

> Rabbi Meir said: When a person is tormented, in what manner does the Divine Presence express itself? "My head is very heavy and aching, My arms are heavy and aching." If this is the pained response of the Almighty when the blood of the wicked is spilt, is it not even more greatly anguished when the blood of the righteous is spilt? (*Sanhedrin 46a*)

5. Rabbi Moshe Feinstein, *Iggerot Moshe* (Brooklyn: Moriah, 1959), Y.D. I, #224, p. 455.

God's head and arms ache from grief. It is a challenge to re-create history and feel the emotions of others, but if God can do it, then acting in the image of God, so must we.

We are called upon to relive history repeatedly throughout the year. We tell the story of our exodus as if it happened yesterday, and we are the victors. We sit in *sukkot* to relive the trials and triumphs of our ancestors. We weep at our loss as if we sat in Jerusalem and watched the flames ourselves. In the words of Rabbi Haskel Lookstein, "It is not ancient history; it is a contemporary experience. This is the approach of the Jew to all of our history and its recollections in all of our festivals."[6]

Our generation has an additional challenge in relating to this saddest day of the Jewish year. There is a modern State of Israel where the three-thousand-year-old city of Jerusalem is a crown of architectural beauty, not a place of ruin. The prayer that the *Shulḥan Arukh* asks of us when we see Jerusalem in a state of destruction has every place in the Tisha B'Av liturgy – until you actually find yourself reciting *Eikha* in Jerusalem's Old City. There can be no arguing that Israel is still vulnerable and its security still a cause for constant concern, but few can deny the paradox that so many lines in *Eikha* present. The book's very opening seems a contradiction to the Jerusalem that we know:

> How does the city sit solitary, that was full of people!
> How is she become like a widow!
> She that was great among the nations, and princess among the
> provinces,
> How is she become a vassal!
> She weeps sore in the night, and her tears are on her cheeks:
> Among all her lovers she has none to comfort her…
>
> (Lamentations 1:1–2)

Today we do stand to comfort her, thousands of people of all ages, from the full spectrum of religious expression, residents and tourists, gathered

---

6. In Rabbi Haskel Lookstein's "Recollection," *The Koren Mesorat HaRav Kinot* (Jerusalem: OU Press/Koren Publishers Jerusalem, 2010), xxix.

within her walls and outside of them. She is hardly a lonely city. She is a city bustling with people. And yet, the remains of the Temple consist of only one standing outer wall that has become the focus of Jewish prayer the world over. We still have a burning need to understand the scale of the *Mikdash*'s dimensions and to imagine it and rebuild it to its former state of glory. We do not know what it is like to have the Temple as our spiritual focus. We have lost the connection to God, to the altar of forgiveness and thanksgiving that was achievable only within its walls.

There are those who – to experience the day of Tisha B'Av – force themselves to contemporize it. In addition to the traditional prayers of the period, they read testimonies of Israeli soldiers in captivity or accounts of Holocaust survivors; they watch documentaries of painful periods of Jewish history. They try hard to overcome the psychological dissonance by emotionally generating feelings that are related in kind, and possibly degree, to that for which we mourn. Strictly speaking, these too are distractions. Meaningful distractions are still distractions. They do not have the *Mikdash* at their core, and it is the Temple's existence that is the primary focus of our *avelut*, our mourning. Everything else is of only secondary or tertiary importance, coming in the wake of the Temple's destruction. Focusing on other tragedies may help achieve the same emotional outcome but is missing the point. It is the equivalent of a child who loses a parent but does not feel the requisite emotions; because he knows he *should* feel and look sad, he thinks of the loss of something else. He may be genuinely despondent but no one could claim, least of all him, that he is mourning a parent.

The words of *Eikha* make the primary focus unmistakable.

> Judah is gone into exile because of affliction, and because of
> great servitude…
> The ways of Zion do mourn, because none come to the solemn
> assembly:
> all her gates are desolate: her priests sigh… (Lam. 1:3–4)

The city is empty; the roads are deserted. The priests are despondent. The texts of the day help us visualize the loss. The book of Jeremiah also demands that when we look at the destruction of the Temple, we meditate on our own accountability for these tragedies and do not merely place them at the feet of our enemies.

> In those days, and in that time, says the Lord, the children of Israel shall come, they and the children of Judah together, going and weeping: they shall go, and seek the Lord their God. They shall ask the way to Zion with their faces towards it, saying, Come, and let us join ourselves to the Lord in a perpetual covenant that shall not be forgotten. (Jeremiah 50:4–5)

These few verses from Jeremiah give us a quick sweep of history – the tears and the reconciliation, the hiding and the seeking, the loss of face and the change of facial direction toward Zion. Ultimately, Jeremiah prophesies, we will form an unbreakable attachment, entering a covenant that will never be forgotten. Attachment always precedes covenant. The emotion creates the bond, and the covenant seals the bond in perpetuity.

During the Three Weeks and Tisha B'Av, we do not only bemoan a recurring past. We also stand in a spiritually secure place, in the presence of community, and ask ourselves the existential questions that every individual and community must ask. And when we sit on the floor and follow the haunting melody of *Eikha*, we pause at the second-to-last verse. It is read by the congregation as a whole, and then repeated again at the conclusion: "Turn us to You, O Lord, and we shall be turned; renew our days as of old" (Lam. 5:21). We close with a plea – take us back. Reconcile. Bring us to the love and longing that we once had, as individuals to our God, as a nation to our sacred spaces, and as a people to our land, Zion.

ALLOWING MEMORY TO SPEAK

Jews are beings of memory. Thus far, we have spoken only of the importance of reliving history. But something more intimate beckons. Within each of us is held a long personal and communal history dating back to the days of Abraham. Each step we take is over four thousand years old. It is hard to move in that vast, complex universe without a sense of how history informs our very identity. Job once asked, "But where shall wisdom be found? And where is the place of understanding?" (28:12). The wisdom and understanding that Job seeks lie in a combination of memory and mystery. We are because we remember. We build a future based on a web of patterns and behaviors generated over centuries. Yet in our history there are inexplicable gaps, miracles of survival and stories of unfathomable pain that are difficult to believe. That is why memory is so central to the Jewish experience. No one would believe us if we were not witnesses to our own past.

There is no real word in Hebrew for history, only for memory: *zakhor*. As Yosef Yerushalmi reminds us:

> Memory is always problematic, usually deceptive, sometimes treacherous...we ourselves are periodically aware that memory is among the most fragile and capricious of our faculties.[7]

Memory implies something far more personal than history; it is the living presence of a people's triumphs and despairs that we carry with us internally wherever we are, not a historic catalogue of activities listed in some other, distant, impersonal space. Elie Wiesel once said, "Because I remember, I despair. Because I remember I have the duty to reject despair" (Nobel Lecture, 11 December 1986). Jewish history is a story of the impossible. Carried within each of us is the touchstone of the impossible when we face despair. We can overcome. We have overcome. When we review our past, we reject despair because we can sum it up in one word: hope.

At no time in the Jewish calendar is this better expressed than on Tisha B'Av. To personalize this tragedy, we refer to the specific acts of destruction as *Ḥurban HaBayit*, the destruction of *the* House. The *Beit HaMikdash* becomes, in our vast collective memory, the loss of the ultimate House, the joint, cherished space that once defined our relationship with God, that shaped the habits and particulars of religious life for centuries and that provided us with a spiritual center, no matter where we were located. The *Mikdash* was not only the location of our divine stirrings and our loftiest aspirations, it also mirrored the very way we speak of God. God is *HaMakom*, the Place, the nexus of space and time

7. Yosef Hayim Yerushalmi, *Zakhor: Jewish History and Jewish Memory* (Seattle: University of Washington Press, 1982), p. 5.

precisely because God transcends both, but we do not. We are limited, finite, situated. As a result, the *Mikdash* becomes a critical address for finding the *Makom*. Yet it is near impossible to mourn a loss if we have little sense of what we are mourning. What is the significance of the Temple, the *Mikdash*, such that its loss stirs our grief?

GOD'S HOUSE

In the very physical, situated state of being human, we choose to refer to the *Mikdash* as a home, the repository of intimate love, as we read in Psalms: "Lord, I love the habitation of Your house, and the place where Your glory dwells. (Psalms 26:8). Calling it the House is not calling it a synagogue; a house escapes the institutionalization implied by a building. It creates an image of warmth and invitation. It welcomes us to enter the personal space of the Other, with all of its subterranean complexities: "For My House shall be called a house of prayer for all peoples," says Isaiah of God's expansiveness (Isaiah 56:7). All who enter are invited to be "joyful in My house of prayer" (ibid.). This locus of international petition and supplication is not denied to anyone who chooses to make the *Mikdash* a platform for his or her sincerest offerings.

Before there was a *Mikdash* there was a *Mishkan*; a portable dwelling before there was a permanent home. Its creation became the group project of our fledging nation; all were to contribute their resources and talents. It was built in the wilderness where material objects are scarce and where God is generally to be found in nature rather than in a tented, purpose-built dwelling. Yet God states through the agency of Moses: "And let them make Me a sanctuary that I may dwell among them" (Exodus 25:8). Commentators on this famous verse are quick to point out the misalignment of subject and predicate. It should say, "Make Me a sanctuary that I may dwell in *it*." Instead, we find an alternative understanding of what it means to bring God down from the heavens to an earthly abode. Build a house so that God can live in *you*. The very attempt to create a place for the *Shekhina*, the Divine Presence, will help you transcend any human notion of place, and bring you closer to the Holy One.

Timing is everything when you build a house. If we look at a large swath of Exodus, we encounter a pattern made familiar to us through the words of the philosopher Martin Buber. Buber's famous

I–Thou relationship is manifest in the tribulations of God and the ancient Israelites. In Egypt, Israelite slavery distanced our people from the integrity and dignity of faith. Slowly, over the period of the plagues, Moses removed the Israelites from the Egyptians' mindset, and helped them appreciate the power and goodness of the One God in a country immersed in the I–It orientation of pagan worship, where gods and people become objects. Yet when the people arrived at Sinai, they encountered a God whose voice was so fear-inducing that they requested that the commandments be delivered solely through the agency of Moses. Set to the backdrop of lightning, thunder, smoke and the increasingly loud sound of the shofar, the scene was overwhelming; warnings to back away from the Mount on pain of death augmented the awe and fearfulness of the encounter. Moses feared nothing, but the people feared everything and held themselves back: "And the people stood afar off, and Moses drew near to the thick darkness where God was" (Exodus 20:18). All in all, God appears as everything, as the people shrink into nothing.

Seen in this context, it should be no surprise that in Exodus 32, only a dozen chapters after the revelation at Mount Sinai, the Israelites built a golden calf. Feeling that God was everything and they were nothing, they were now bent on reversing the terms – another manifestation of the I–It relationship, a confrontation of needs and wants rather than authentic relationship.

Only with Moses' request for forgiveness and the building of the *Mishkan* is there the beginning of genuine intimacy, an I–Thou encounter. And when the *Mishkan* is completed, we read that "the Presence of the Lord filled the Tabernacle" (Exodus 40:34), and with that Presence, there was no room left for human labor or human presence. "And Moses was not able to enter the Tent of Meeting, because the cloud rested on it, and the Presence of the Lord filled the tabernacle" (40:35). But a Tent of Meeting is only useful if those who occupy it can *meet* the Other. Thus begins the book of Leviticus, devoted to the details of worship in the *Mishkan*, "And the Lord called to Moses and spoke to him out of the Tent of Meeting…" (Leviticus 1:1). God did fill the *Mishkan* but then, in what the mystics would call *tzimtzum*, divine contraction, He created a place for humans in His House, a true meeting place, a location for the I–Thou.

This spiritual center was a necessary anchor at a time of ambivalence, anxiety and loss of direction that our ancestors experienced in the wilderness. In Numbers, we find that the reconstruction of the *Mishkan* in each location had to be duplicated with precision; wherever the Israelites encamped, the *Mishkan* had to be built exactly as it was built the very first time. True to its metaphoric role as the camp's center, it was also in the literal center of the camp, with attendant priests and Levites representing the first tiers to encamp around it, flanked by the rest of the tribes. When it came time to move, the *Mishkan* was first to be taken apart; and when it came time to set up camp, the *Mishkan* was first to be put up. Its movement signaled the movement of the entire camp: "When the Tabernacle sets forward, the Levites shall take it down; and when the Tabernacle is to be pitched, the Levites shall set it up" (Numbers 1:51). Between the surety of slavery and the anticipation of homeland, we had only one center that offered us security at a time of insecurity: God's portable House.

Much later, when we reached our homeland and secured our borders, King David initiates the building of the *Mikdash* precisely after reflecting on the human need for shelter:

> When the king was settled in his palace and the Lord had granted him safety from all the enemies around him, the king said to the prophet Nathan: 'Here I am dwelling in a house of cedar, while the Ark of the Lord abides in a tent!'" (II Samuel 7:1–2)

Consumed with guilt that he lived in a home while God "lived" in a tent, David wanted to build the Ark a permanent home where the beauty of its contents would be matched by its aesthetic covering, not by flimsy cloth walls. When the *Mikdash* was finally completed by David's son Solomon, the new king offered his benediction by exploring the contradictory notion of place in the constellation of holiness:

> O Lord, God of Israel, in the heavens above and in the earth below there is no god like You...But will God really dwell on earth? Even the heavens to their uttermost reaches cannot contain You, how much less this House that I have built...May Your

eyes be open day and night toward this House, toward the place of which You have said: My name shall abide there … give heed in Your heavenly abode, give heed and pardon. (1 Kings 8:23–30)

King Solomon opened this new chapter in the life of our people by reflecting on the irony of containing God in a dwelling, a house, when God can never be limited by human dimensions of space. We are human. These limitations are all we understand.

Thus, the loss of this ultimate House, *Hurban HaBayit*, can only be understood through the loss of its microcosm, our own homes. Imagine a fire sweeping through every room of your house, taking with it in its destructive path the family portraits, the dinner table that served up so many intimate memories, the stores of souvenirs, objects and furniture that make up a life. In our sentimental moments, each nook and corner holds reservoirs of meaning. Who am I if I no longer have a home? Often when people are moving and look at the contents of their homes boxed up in cartons, their houses stripped of personal identifying markers, they experience the existential dizziness of dislocation. Imagine now that we undergo this as an entire people. We don't know who we are when our center is removed.

Contemporary novelist Nicole Krauss beautifully captures this fundamental national loss through the nostalgia of one of her characters:

> Two thousand years have passed, my father used to tell me, and now every Jewish soul is built around the house that burned in that fire, so vast that we can, each one of us, only recall the tiniest fragment: a pattern on the wall, a knot in the wood of a door, a memory of how light fell across the floor. But if every Jewish memory were put together, every last holy fragment joined up as one, the House would be built again … or rather a memory of the House so perfect that it would be, in essence, the original itself. Perhaps that is what they mean when they speak of the Messiah: a perfect assemblage of the infinite parts of the Jewish memory.[8]

---

8. Nicole Krauss, *Great House* (New York: W.W. Norton and Company, 2010), p. 279.

But we are far, so far, from having the safety of that perfect memory. God's world, not only ours, contracted in the ashes of destruction. The God who has dominion over all, lost a touch-point to humanity. This shrinking of the sacred is what we mourn. The collapse of beauty, the sudden inwardness of our tradition, the move from the altar to the mind as the focus of Jewish life, all of these were sacrificed in much the same way that the *Mikdash* once functioned to hold our guilt- and thanksgiving-offerings. We mourn a Judaism we never knew, one we can only imagine – the sights and smells, the bustle of pilgrimage, the relief of expiation, the reunion of families, the ingathering of people around a shared dream. We give a metaphoric nod in that direction when we pray: post-destruction, the Mishna canonized the original dream by instructing that we pray only in the direction of the *Mikdash*. The tractate of *Berakhot* (4:6) advises us to turn our hearts to the chamber of the Holy of Holies, and the *Tosefta* there (3:15) follows with its mandate to pray in the direction of Jerusalem and the Temple from wherever we are in the world. The Temple in its absence can only receive the vibrations of our once national heart, directed in totality to a spot where few Jews can set foot today.

MARKING DESTRUCTION

In our search for language to capture Ḥurban, destruction, we turn to *Eikha*; there we find the expression that has become eponymous with this time period of mourning: "Judah has gone into exile because of misery and harsh oppression; when she settled among the nations, she found no rest; all her pursuers overtook her in the narrow places" (1:3). The period of the Three Weeks, which spans the time from the initial siege of ancient Jerusalem to the destruction of the city and its Temple, is called "the narrow places" or *Bein HaMitzarim,* after this early verse from the book of Lamentations. Others translate the expression as "between the narrow straits," indicating the vulnerable place between two pieces of land that connotes desolation, exposure, and intractability. These narrow spaces must be passed through to get from one place to another but are rarely regarded as stopping grounds. They signify exile and banishment, a place that is neither here nor there, an area almost absent of its own identity. The narrowness in the rabbinic mind, however, is not of space but of time.

In order to return us to this period of time in the imagination, the sages of the Talmud established a number of laws to frame and recreate the experience of tragedy. Just as mourning over a person is ritually divided into different grieving periods – the time before burial, the day of the burial, the week after burial, the month after burial, the year of mourning and then the annual marking of the death – so, too, does Jewish law divide national mourning into different grieving segments. It begins with the 17th of Tammuz, *Shiva Asar B'Tammuz*, mid-way into the Hebrew month of Tammuz, which is the initial fast that ushers in the period. It is a minor fast, a fast which begins in the morning rather than the night before.

The first mention of this fast is in the book of Zechariah 8:19. It appears as one of a series of fast days marking tragedy which, in the messianic era, will be transformed to joyous celebrations. Officially, it is the opening of the season of mourning because the siege of Jerusalem's walls during *Bayit Sheni*, the Second Temple, began on this day. But the Talmudic sages identified an additional four tragedies that happened on this day: Moses broke the two tablets containing the Ten Command-ments, an idol was erected in the Temple's inner sanctum, the twice-daily sacrifice offered on the Temple's altar was discontinued, and a Roman military leader, Apostomus, burned a Torah scroll.[9]

The fact that all of these tragedies befell the Jewish people dur-ing the same annual period is religiously significant. Certain days or seasons are dangerous or inopportune. We often avoid difficult days on the calendar or fear their impending approach not because we are certain that they will prove difficult in the future, but because they were troublesome in the past. Such anniversaries of doom fill us with anxiety. On the recurring day of the calendar that marks the loss of a loved one, a near-fatal accident, or the diagnosis of a life-threatening illness, we may intentionally choose not to do something joyous because it may feel like a betrayal of the past or a personal insult to the person we lost. That is not superstitious; it is a respect for the passage of time and the events that color it.

The Three Weeks are no exception. We enter a somber frame of

9. Mishna *Ta'anit* 4:6.

mind. Jewish law frowns upon engagement in risky behavior during the Nine Days before Tisha B'Av, and even more so during the week in which Tisha B'Av falls, because history did not look kindly at the Jews at this hour. Some people avoid activities that they personally deem dangerous. Naturally, at such a somber time, joyous functions are avoided. Public celebrations, parties and other festive activities are not scheduled in these weeks. Weddings are not held. Attendance at live concerts is prohibited. New homes are not purchased; new clothing is not bought. Many people do not listen to music that may make them light-hearted and happy. As in the mourning for the passing of a relative, men generally refrain from shaving, and both men and women do not cut their hair. In the same vein, during the Nine Days, as the fast day approaches, people customarily do not launder or iron clothing unless it is particularly soiled and needs to be washed immediately. In commemoration of the lost Temple sacrifices, we also refrain from eating meat. Certain Sephardic practices limit these restrictions to the actual week in which Tisha B'Av occurs.

Altogether, these practices impinge very little on the larger experience of life. Rather, they are meant to punctuate the mundane aspects of daily living: what we wear, how we eat, who we are with and why. Cleanliness, freshness, satiation and newness are all minimized in some fashion to help us achieve the demanding mood of the season, the sense of loss.

The prohibition of "newness" itself requires exploration. Judaism celebrates newness and wonder. The blessing of *Sheheheyanu* hails significant new points in time, or the acquisition of a new item. Because the recitation of this blessing marks some element of renewal and joy, we usually refrain from any activity or significant purchase which would engender happiness and necessitate the blessing during the Three Weeks. For example, we do not eat new fruit (fruit that has not been tasted for more than thirty days), nor buy or wear new clothing. We avoid large purchases and home renovations. These projects all signal anticipation and positive change. Our spiritual task for this small clutch of time is to be more moderate in our expression of happiness.

The Talmud says that just as we are to increase our happiness – our *simha* – in the month of Adar in which Purim falls, we are to minimize our happiness when Av begins. There is a Hasidic rendering of this expression, attributed to Rabbi Menachem Mendel Schneerson, which reinterprets the Talmudic maxim: *"Mi shenikhnas Av, mematim – besimḥa,* As Av approaches, we minimize – with happiness." The simple placement of a pause, a break, changes the entire reading. We minimize the self, but even that we do with joy.

While all of the behaviors mandated by the Talmud temper joy, they also help us understand the definition of joy from a Jewish legal perspective. Happiness is not only or primarily measured by material success, personal achievement or status; it is found in the small acts of beauty and compassion that comprise a life. Today, in a time of such consumer excess, it is hard to get excited over the purchase of a suit or a dress, the tasting of an exotic fruit after a month or two without one, or the sound of live music heard in the company of friends. Our sense of wonder has been lost. But this period reminds us that these small plea-sures in the aggregate are the measure of life's happiness, the mosaic of pleasure that buoys us day in and day out. Perhaps we only appreciate the wonder in their absence.

THE PRICE OF DESTRUCTION

With every loss of sacred space comes a narrowing of identity. With the loss of the *Beit HaMikdash* we became less of who we were and who we wanted to be. Tragedy has that impact. Along with the destruction of buildings and the death of human beings, the Three Weeks mark changes in the existential psyche of the Jewish people. The destruction of Jerusalem and its sanctuaried centerpiece gave rise to an alternate route to God – sacred study. This relatively new and intensified spiri-tual occupation arose because one sage, Rabbi Yoḥanan ben Zakkai, escaped Jerusalem's walls through a ruse and asked the newly declared Roman emperor, Vespasian: "Give me Yavne and its scholars."[10] He took a religious risk, and gave up the larger dream of saving Jerusalem for a more-likely-to-be-granted boon of an insignificant town not very far away. There he hoped that he and a small group of surviving rabbis could move the spiritual center of Judaism temporarily away from Jeru-salem and its Temple practices. He reluctantly forfeited priests for rabbis,

10. *Gittin* 56b.

altars for Jewish law and pilgrimages of the body for journeys of the mind. Consequently, he dramatically changed the Jewish present and future.

The preeminence of learning in this new mode of Pharisaic existence required a marketing plan and salesman, to speak prosaically; it was difficult to forego the tangible benefits of Temple service, the atonement and celebration through sacrifice, for the more abstract and ethereal benefits of study. One scholar in the Talmudic sea remarked that "Since the Temple was destroyed, all God has in this universe is four cubits of Jewish law" (*Berakhot* 8a). This measurement is a standard rabbinic measurement demarcating personal space. It is virtually impossible to conceptualize the fact that once the majestic Temple was gone, God went from possessing a universe, to "owning" only the equivalent of six feet of a study hall. Again, the experience of exile and destruction changed us. It narrowed us. It even narrowed our perception of God's space in our world.

It is easy, therefore, to understand Jewish mourning centuries earlier. In the book of Jeremiah, we find multiple verses that communicate physical anguish. Israel is regarded as a slave who is continually exposed to violence: "Lions have roared over him, have raised their cries. They have made his land a waste. His cities desolate, without inhabitants" (Jeremiah 2:15). In addition to the external pressures of enemies is the pressing question of internal worthiness. Did we deserve a sacred space for the Divine Presence? Was the destruction of Jerusalem a statement of distance between God and the Jewish people? Did we create a loving environment toward God and others that would make the *Mikdash* capable of offering redemption? These questions haunt Jeremiah:

Roam the streets of Jerusalem. Search its squares. Look about and take note; you will not find a man. There is none who acts justly, who seeks integrity that I should pardon her...Oh Lord, Your eyes look for integrity. You have struck them, but they sensed no pain. (Jeremiah 5:1–3)

Jeremiah's Jerusalem is not ravaged by enemies; it is brought low by the absence of integrity of its own inhabitants. God makes the residents of Jerusalem suffer so that they will look in the mirror, but they do not heed the divine moral signal. The wake-up alarm does not work. There is no self-awareness, just an intensification of sin until it inures people to the cause of their own misfortune. It is not coincidental that *Eikha* also offers this sage advice: "Let us search and try our ways, and turn back to the Lord. Let us lift up our hearts with our hands to God in the heavens" (Lam. 3:40–41). The tender image of post-Temple sacrifice is to take one's own heart and offer it in one's hands.

In the middle of *Eikha*, the tone changes. Jeremiah does not lash out at the enemy as much as ask his own followers to give heed, to pay attention to their own actions. Most of all, he advises them to be patient and to create a route to redemption through self-knowledge:

> The Lord is good to those who wait for Him, to the soul that seeks Him. It is good that a man should quietly hope for the salvation of the Lord. It is good for a man that he bear the yoke in his youth. Let him sit alone and keep silence, because he has taken it upon him. Let him put his mouth in the dust; perhaps there may be hope. (Ibid. 3:25–28)

The biblical text stresses waiting, patience and isolation. Waiting is an inherent part of the redemptive process. We err and then pick ourselves up and stumble again. We wait for God to help us. In isolation, we have the quiet and the absence of distraction so that we may face ourselves in our dark hours. If we are patient and able to put our mouths to the dust metaphorically, then there is hope that we will have the humility and honesty to confront adversity and to learn from it.

THIS BOOK

This book provides a short essay for each day of the Three Weeks, to help us understand what we lost so that we can mourn with greater feeling. Most of the essays have their basis in biblical texts read on the Sabbaths and fast days of the season rather than in texts with a halakhic orientation. Some use the book of *Eikha* or the *kinot* as a starting point, others a piece of *aggada* (rabbinic legends and parables). Jeremiah and Isaiah feature prominently throughout as the prophets of doom and consolation: their texts are central to the season. Most, if not all, of the essays focus on our relationship to God, largely because the *Mikdash* was one important avenue to reaching the *Shekhina* or Divine Presence, a connection we now profoundly miss. Many Jews today, even committed, observant Jews, do not engage in God-talk. Perhaps these essays will help us along in these conversations.

Each essay is followed by a *Kavana*, a specific spiritual focus for the day that involves reflection, imagination or action to integrate the learning. These weeks, somber as they are, present an exciting and important time for personal growth and introspection. As *Eikha* itself teaches: "Let us search and examine our ways, and turn back to the Lord" (3:40).

And, as is the Jewish way, the twenty-one pieces on the Three Weeks, and the essay for Tisha B'Av, are concluded with a final message of hope and rebuilding for the day after Tisha B'Av. As Jews, we never dwell on the persecutions of the past without opening our arms wide to the promise of the future. Rabbi Soloveitchik once questioned the implications of a midrash on Genesis 1 that states that God created worlds and obliterated them before arriving at our story of creation. He answered that "A Jew has to know how to emulate God, and, like God, to continue to create even after his former world has been eradicated."[11] It is that persistent sense of hope and re-creation despite suffering and destruction that gives us the strength to remember and to transform memory into action, misery into repentance, and desolation into redemption.

---

11. Aaron Rakeffet-Rothkoff, *The Rav: The World of Rabbi Joseph B. Soloveitchik*, Vol. 11 (Jersey City, NJ: KTAV Publishing House, 1999), p. 16.

Day One: 17 Tammuz

FAST OF SHIVA ASAR B'TAMMUZ

Seeking God

Do we achieve holiness, *kedusha*, through seeking God or through finding God? To answer this question, we turn to one of our sacred texts. The *haftara* for Minḥa, the afternoon service, on a fast day is an excerpt from Isaiah 55. It begins mid-chapter, at verse six and closes in the next chapter, verse eight. It contains some of the most religiously inspiring language in all of prophetic literature.

"Seek God where He can be found. Call to Him while He is near" (Isaiah 55:6). Isaiah offers wise, spiritual advice that is no less applicable to God than it is to all of our relationships. Reach out to God in a place where holiness can be found, when God feels near. Use the fast day as a mechanism for the contraction of the material and physical to create a greater space for the *Shekhina*, the Divine Presence. The tone of the day invites greater awareness of God. But Isaiah did not utter these words for a fast day; its incorporation into the service was a later adaptation of a text to enhance the day's emotional demands.

What did the prophet mean when he pronounced these words? Perhaps Isaiah spoke from his awareness that God's presence was not always apparent during the average working day of an Israelite. Busy with harvesting fields, winnowing on the threshing floor or finding a fertile place to graze sheep, our ancestors could have spent their days preoccupied with the demands of family and making a living, not making a place for God. If this was a challenge for those who worked outside in nature every day, imagine how much greater an obstacle today's work environment presents to those of us who sit in offices all day. Without creating a clearing for God, a time and place for thinking above and beyond life's prosaic cares, how can we expect to find Him? If we are not searching, then that which we do not look for can hardly be expected to make itself known. It is like playing hide-and-seek and then not looking. The Kotzker Rebbe, Rabbi Menachem Mendel Morgensztern (1787–1859) once poignantly remarked, "God is where you let Him in."[1]

Isaiah continues to exhort his listeners, offering them both a reason that God may seem hidden and some sound advice about creating room for God:

> Let the wicked give up his ways, the sinful man his plans. Let him turn back to the Lord, and he will pardon him to our God, for He freely forgives. **For My plans are not your plans, nor are My ways your ways** – declares the Lord. But as the heavens are high above the earth, so are My ways high above your ways and My plans above your plans. (Isaiah 55:7–9)

God is not like human beings – "My plans are not your plans" – in that God grants true forgiveness. If we genuinely make room for God, God will make room for us.

Human relationships do not always offer that degree of reciprocity. They are more like the gazelles of the Song of Songs. When one is ready to mate, the other cannot be found. One appears at the door to find the other asleep. When the sleeping one wakes, the other is already gone. This back-and-forth game of emotional hide-and-seek can prove exceptionally frustrating. Our own willingness to start afresh, to forgive,

---

1. As cited in Melinda Ribner, *Everyday Kabbalah: A Practical Guide to Jewish Meditation, Healing, and Personal Growth* (Secaucus, NJ: Citadel Press, 1998).

to seek forgiveness, may or may not be matched in the mind and heart of someone else. God, on the other hand, is poised and waiting for us when – and only when – we finally make room for God in our lives; when we are compassionate, forgiving, thoughtful people.

Among commentators, there is a division between those who regard seeking God as a challenge of time and those who consider it a challenge of space. Either certain times create the possibility of holiness, or certain places do. Rashi, citing a midrash, identifies a moment in time that is ripe for relationship with God: "Before the verdict takes place, when He still says to you, 'Seek Me.'"[2] Seek God before life gets difficult, when God is reaching out to you, do not wait till things go wrong. There are always moments of tenderness in a relationship that should be enlarged, leveraged, expanded. Respond to those moments. Sometimes we let go too soon. We had the chance to say something that needed to be said, and the moment presented itself, but we let it go. There was a kind word or a compliment that should have been uttered, but wasn't. It's true in sacred times with others and also with God. There was a word of praise or gratitude we could have said in our *tefillot*, prayers, that we let slip away, or an apology that might have brought us closer to God, but we weren't seeking and so we lost it. If you're not looking then you won't find God.

The second-century Aramaic translation of the text, *Targum Yonatan*, embellishes this reading in its paraphrase: "Pray to God while you are still alive." Repent while you can, not when it is too late to fix what is broken. And so much is broken.

In an interesting Talmudic interpretation, King Manasseh, who ruled in Isaiah's day, challenged this prophecy, saying that it contradicted something that Moses himself taught. In Deuteronomy, Moses tells the people that God responds whenever people call to Him.[3] Should we seek God where God is or does God respond to us where we are? The Talmud reconciles this contradiction by saying that Moses was referring to communal repentance which is always accepted, whereas Isaiah's pleas are for individual repentance, which has greater effectiveness during the

2. *Sifrei, Naso* 42.
3. Deuteronomy 4:7.

ten days between Rosh HaShana and Yom Kippur.[4] There are specific times in the calendar year that nurture repentance. Seek God during those times, when the very air seems ready for transformation. But if you are part of a community then any time works since the power of seeking God in community is stronger.

The readings above interpret "where He is found" as a reference to time, but there are also readings that relate the search to place. According to the great medieval commentator Abraham Ibn Ezra, the verse refers to a changed historical reality: Once Isaiah predicted salvation from Babylon and the removal of the bonds of exile, the people could finally imagine finding God back in the land of Israel. Exile wears us down, leaving little time or mental space to engage in spiritual pursuits. Israel becomes *the* place to search for God.

The Jerusalem Talmud, in contrast, sees the place-of-finding as referring to synagogues and study halls.[5] There are spaces that are specifically designated for spiritual behaviors and rituals, and these locations stir us to seek God. In the kinetic energy of a room full of genuine religious feeling or of people exchanging ideas, you can find God more easily. In between the pews of a synagogue, among people immersed in prayer, in the lofty sanctuaries that we build, we can make more room for God. Imagine being in a synagogue at night when all the people are gone and only the eternal light – the *ner tamid* – is alight. There is something holy about that place: the small flame in the big space, the darkness that removes visual distractions, the weight of silence – all of it signals transcendence.

It is not easy to predict where God is to be found, so sometimes we can fulfill Isaiah's demand by identifying where God is *not* in our lives. We know that there are specific times when we feel too anxious to pray or too preoccupied with mundane chores and the needs of others to seek God. There are also places where it seems impossible to focus. There is too much going on, or too many people talking, or too much havoc for us to find God. Seek God in places not only where God is likely to be found but also where *you* are most receptive to God's presence. Recep-

4. *Yevamot* 49b.
5. Jerusalem Talmud, *Berakhot* 5:1.

tivity can happen in the least likely of places. An open heart helps the spiritual seeker keep all possibilities present and ready. We may never find God, but the search brings us closer.

Kavana for the Day

Seeking is about discovery. Isaiah tells us to seek God where God is to be found. Think about where you might find God. People have a custom to pray and study in a *"makom kavua,"* a fixed location or place, every day. The idea is that we create spaces that are receptive to spiritual activities, where we have all that we need: the right light, the right balance of privacy and companionship, the right amount of noise or silence to induce spiritual behaviors. Think hard. Where does God seem most apparent in your life? What times and places seem more open and receptive to spiritual seeking and finding? Recreate those times and spaces and make your own *makom kavua.*

Day Two: 18 Tammuz
Fighting Job's Demons

Torah study is regarded as a pleasure of high order. Consequently, its study is forbidden on Tisha B'Av precisely because of the mental enjoyment it confers. And yet, there are certain texts that we are permitted to learn on this mournful day, and the book of Job is among them. Tucked deep in the Tanakh, the Job narrative is one of the premier texts of the Three Weeks with which few of us are personally acquainted.

Job, regarded by some traditional commentators as a fictitious character[1] created to teach us profound lessons in faith and loyalty, was sorely tested. He was a man who had everything: a loving family, financial success, friendship and respect within his community. Satan challenged

---

1. In addition to medieval commentators like Joseph Kaspi who treated Job as a fiction, the historicity of Job as a real character is argued as early as the Talmud: *Bava Batra* 15a, where an anonymous rabbi argues against R. Shmuel bar Naḥmani that Job "never was and never existed." Resh Lakish supports this view in the Jerusalem Talmud, *Sota* 20c and *Bereshit Raba* 57:4. An excellent discussion of this issue is found in Robert Eisen's *The Book of Job in Medieval Jewish Philosophy* (New York: Oxford University Press, 2004).

God on the grounds of belief. People are God-fearing when luck travels their way. It is easy to be faithful and grateful when God's bounty is felt as a daily presence. But what would happen, Satan goaded God, if everything that was wonderful about Job's life was incrementally taken away? Would Job remain a faithful servant?

As readers, aware as Job is not of Satan's ruse, we watch sadly as Job undergoes profound loss. He is struck at every turn with sickness and death. He gradually loses everything that comprises personal identity. We hear Job's anguish. It is great poetry, and we feel strange savoring the way he articulates anguish as one of the finest in the face of loss:

> Job began to speak and cursed the day of his birth. Job spoke up and said:
>> Perish the day I was born and the night it was announced that a male had been conceived.
>> May that day be darkness;
>> May God above have no concern for it;
>> May light not shine on it;
>> May darkness and deep gloom reclaim it;
>> May a pall lie over it;
>> May what blackens the day terrify it.
>> May obscurity carry off that night;
>> May it not be counted among the days of the year;
>> May it not appear in any of its months;
>> May that night be desolate;
>> May no sound of joy be heard upon it. (Job 3:1–7)

Job begs the heavens to eliminate him, to erase all thoughts of him, undoing his very creation and any mention of it. The day should be erased from history so that it can be as naught. And yet, despite Job's wish to vanquish himself and rewrite his story, he does not for a moment question God's existence. He questions his own. One thing remains a constant that Job never loses – his faith in God. Satan tries, but Satan fails. Job continues to believe in his Maker even when his Maker seems to reject him. Elie Wiesel, another person who could easily have lost his faith, writes, "I am not at peace. I never said I lost my faith in God. I was angry. I still don't understand God's ways."[2]

Job struggles to understand why his life has taken such a catastrophic downfall.

> Summon me and I will respond.
> Or I will speak and You will reply to me.
> How many are my iniquities and sins?
> Advise me of my transgression and sin.
> Why do You hide Your face
> And treat me like an enemy?...
> Man wastes away like a rotten thing,
> Like a garment eaten by moths. (Job 13: 22–28)

We sense the enormity of Job's despair. He tries desperately to understand, and implores God to explain his change of circumstances – to show Job his own accountability. He does not run away from the brutal truths about his own transgressions. He invites God to list them so that he can make sense of his world.

Eliphaz, Job's supposed friend, magnifies Job's anguish by telling him that he must have done something to deserve what is happening to him:

> Think now what innocent man ever perished?
> Where have the upright been destroyed?
> As I have seen, those who plow evil
> And sow mischief reap the same.
> They perish by a blast from God,
> Are gone at the breath of His nostrils. (Job 4:7–9)

For Eliphaz, it is simply inconceivable that Job would suffer without

---

2. Elie Wiesel commenting in 1995 on his ongoing personal struggle with making sense of the Holocaust. As cited in Alfred J. Kolatch, *Great Jewish Quotations* (New York: Jonathan David Publishers, 1996), p. 489.

being the cause of his own suffering. Innocent men never perish in Eliphaz's theology. Only those who deserve it experience pain. Those who "plow evil" will feel the consequences of their behavior.

Eliphaz touches a raw nerve in Job. When life is hard, we search for reasons. With heartbreaking effort, we grasp for explanations that are rarely forthcoming. We ask questions that dissipate into the ether. Humans are interpretive beings; we strive to understand our world even when it seems incomprehensible.

Sometimes, we find purpose in our suffering. Finding purpose is not the same as explaining the cause of a problem, although the two are often confused. A mother may never *understand* the loss of a child, but by creating a non-profit organization in the child's memory, may be able to *create* goodness from her pain. It will never bring her child back, but may redeem some of the tragic sadness.

Our need to interpret experience can also lead us to a more potentially problematic arena – the place of Eliphaz, interpreting the pain and difficulty of others. This transgresses the biblical prohibition of *ona'at devarim*, oppressing someone with words. In Leviticus, we read "Do not wrong one another, but fear your Lord, for I am God your Lord" (25:17). The Talmud offers a number of ways to interpret this verse in a specific manner, offering examples of how we can persecute others with our words. Oppression with words takes many forms, from asking the price of an object with no intention of purchasing it, to inviting someone to an event while knowing that that individual cannot attend, or paying with credit when one has the money. From what seem like relatively minor transgressions, the Talmud enters the emotional minefield of truly oppressive words. When we fabricate reasons for someone else's suffering, we not only take an arrogant and smug stance about another's experience, we also deem that person culpable in some way. Nothing could be more oppressive than heaping guilt or blame on top of a victim's pain.

In the remarkable story of Job, it is not only God who causes Job's suffering, it is his friends who augment his anguish by attributing Job's suffering to his own misdeeds. They rhetorically suggest that people never suffer without deserving it. Each of Job's three friends digs deeper into Job's emotional psyche, mapping out a way to understand the world that makes Job the central cause of his own pain.

Job finally wrests the conversation back to his control, delivering his anguished response:

> How long will you vex my soul and break me in pieces with words? These ten times have you reproached me; you are not ashamed that you slight me. And be it indeed that I have been mistaken, my error remains with myself. (Job 19:1–3)

Job then offers a review of how God has lashed out against him, an implicit suggestion to his visitors that they need not reproach him: God has chastised him enough. And then he poses more ultimate questions to the very people who sit in judgment over him:

> All my trusted friends abhor me, and they whom I love are turned against me … Have pity upon me, have pity upon me, O my friends, for the hand of God has touched me. Why do you, like God, persecute me … ? (Job 19:19–22)

In comparing his friends to God, he also suggests how brazen and inappropriate their judgment is – and how little it is needed, given all the calamity he must negotiate. Instead, Job tells them what he truly needs: pity. He asks the compassion of his friends, not their scorn. Imagine the loneliness of a person who confesses that his friends now hate him, and that those who loved him have left him simply because bad things have happened. Compounding the emotional pain is the alienation and isolation instigated by the responses of others.

The Talmud has no tolerance for such individuals as Job's friends, with their moral self-righteousness. It lets us know in unambiguous terms the exact nature of the prohibition to interpret the suffering of others. We are prohibited from reminding someone who has become religiously observant about his or her past; we cannot ask a convert about his parents; we are forbidden to interpret the calamities that have befallen others. Each of these acts exposes another human being's vulnerability in a gaping, painful and raw way. While others may choose to share the past with us, that is to be an act of their personal choice. We are not allowed to open the portals into another's secrets, personal transformation or heartache. Each of the Talmud's prohibitions reveals another element of the multi-layered nature of selfhood.

Verbal oppression gets at the heart of another person's identity. It is an attack on the essential self – on the choices a person has made about how he conducts his life or how he responds to events beyond his control. We must leave that to the dignity of he who has made these choices.

Indeed, the Talmud even suggests that bringing up any aspect of another's past that would cause offense or jog bad emotions is forbidden. We may find ourselves constantly bringing up the past in a debate with a parent, friend, sibling or spouse. We identify patterns in their behavior and then, in a moment of perceived weakness, we throw the pattern at them: "You can never be trusted…You always do that…You did the same thing last week." Last month. Last year. In making these pernicious observations we are minimizing the ability of an individual to change, to renew each day, and locking him into past behaviors and responses.

Job offers us a unique window into the interior of the sufferer, not only so that we can face our own difficulties with a measure of faith, but so that we can be better friends to those who suffer.

Kavana for the Day

Think about a way that you oppressed someone with your words. Just one incident. Now search for a way you can find a *tikkun*, reparation, for that hurt. Heal it by using your words with that same individual today. Oppression is overcome through redemption; one redeeming act at a time. Ask an open-ended question and become a patient, active listener. Become an emotional sounding board in this encounter, not offering judgment, even if asked. Allow silence to hover without feeling the need to punctuate it with talk. Silence is often the most noble, honest and understandable response to suffering. Experience silence together.

Day Three: 19 Tammuz

God's List

We love to make lists, to categorize and organize our complex universe and our responsibilities within it. Somehow, when we make a list, we feel that much closer to achieving our goals. The Talmud understood the power of lists, and at the end of Tractate *Makkot*, we find a historically evolving list of behaviors that sum up the *taryag mitzvot*, the 613 commandments. The Gemara opens with King David, saying that he reduced all of the mitzvot to eleven core ethical principles:

1. Walk in perfect innocence
2. Work righteously
3. Speak the truth from your heart
4. Have no slander on your tongue
5. Do no harm to your fellow
6. Cast no disgrace on someone who is close to you
7. Find no person contemptible
8. Honor those who fear God
9. Keep your word in an oath
10. Lend money without collecting interest

11. Take no bribes against the innocent.[1]

This is a powerful and ambitious list, and the Gemara goes on to illustrate these principles by naming people who embodied these behaviors. But then the Gemara engages in a discussion to reduce the number of core principles. Can the 613 mitzvot be captured in their essence in even fewer principles?

Isaiah is the next candidate; his list consists of only six principles:

1. Walk righteously
2. Speak with fairness
3. Spurn illicit financial gain
4. Take no bribes
5. Seal your ears from hearing of bloodshed
6. Shut your eyes from seeing evil.[2]

The text then elaborates on each of these principles and how to uphold them. But even this number was too large for Ḥazal, the sages, and they reduced the list even further by turning to three principles in the book of Micah:

1. Do justice
2. Love kindness
3. Walk humbly with God.[3]

The Talmudic text sums up by turning back to Isaiah, offering up two core principles as a summation of all of the mitzvot:

1. Observe justice
2. Act with righteousness.[4]

All worship of God is contained in assiduously following these two essen-

---

1. *Makkot* 24a, based on a creative reading of Psalm 15.
2. This is based on a reading of Isaiah 33:15.
3. This is based on Micah 6:8.
4. This reading is based on Isaiah 56:1.

tial values. The rest is commentary. But then the Talmud cites Habakkuk 2:4, reducing all 613 commandments to one ethical requirement: "But the righteous person shall live through his faith."

God, too, has a list. It is not a happy list, a catalogue of the habits of the religious heart. Instead, in the book of Proverbs, *Mishlei*, we find a list of behaviors that God despises, a catalogue of the human weaknesses and failings that keeps us distant from justice and righteousness. This litany gives us insight into the seeds of human integrity, by demonstrating to us the fundamental behaviors that cause it to break down. The text states:

> God hates six things; seven things are an abomination to Him.
> A haughty bearing
> A lying tongue
> Hands that shed innocent blood
> A mind that hatches evil plots
> Feet quick to run to evil
> A false witness testifying lies
> And one who incites brothers to quarrel. (Proverbs 6:16–19)

Even at first glance, we notice that dishonesty is a central component of God's hate list. Dishonesty is closely tied to arrogance. Those who regard themselves as superior hatch plots to make themselves stronger at the expense of others.

The book of Proverbs does not leave us with the ugly aspects of humanity without offering a way to ameliorate the problems identified:

> … keep your father's commandments.
> Do not forsake your mother's teaching.
> Tie them over your heart always.
> Bind them around your throat.
> When you walk it will lead you.
> When you lie down it will watch over you;
> and when you are awake, it will talk with you.
> For the commandment is a lamp,
> the teaching is a light. (Proverbs 6:20–23)

This advice suggests ways to remind ourselves of the disciplines that guide and anchor us. When we focus on something holy, something that offers our lives meaning, we reinforce the good that our hearts truly desire to follow. We find that when we are open about the way this force occupies our lives – when we tie it around our hearts and our throats – it becomes a guide that protects us, talks to us, helps us make decisions. Rather than state the principles as the Talmud does, the book of Proverbs connects us to the ways and means that these principles can impact upon us. They must be with us constantly as reminders, sources of light, and holy teachings.

Kavana for the Day

Make a list of ten principles through which you try to live your life. Now try to reduce it to five. Having done so, try to get the list down to three. How would you remind yourself of these three principles on a daily basis? Think about an object, person or moment that inspires you and keeps you on the straight and narrow. There is a beautiful midrash that tells us that when Joseph was being pursued by Potiphar's wife, he envisioned the face of his father before him to give him strength and remind himself of who he was – not situationally, but continuously, throughout his life. It is easy to compromise ourselves in a moment that makes an everlasting imprint on ourselves and others. A moment. Can a moment ever be more important than a lifetime? This visual aid reinforced the life that Joseph wanted to live and the person he wanted to be, even at a time that sorely tested his soul. How can you harness this object or voice to serve as a constant reminder of what is important to you?

Day Four: 20 Tammuz

A Wayward Child,
an Estranged Parent

Whateter do we do when family relationships fall apart? One of
the texts we read at this season is Isaiah 1:1–27, a *haftara* that centers
around this very theme. Isaiah refers to the children of Israel as literal
children – rebellious, ungrateful, and depraved. God is depicted as a
broken father to these children who refuse to listen. The divine words
echo in the ears of every parent: "Hear O heavens, and give ear, O earth,
for the Lord has spoken: 'I reared children and brought them up – and
they have rebelled against Me!'" (Isaiah 1:2).

God asks heaven and earth to pay attention. God speaks to nature
in the hope that someone is listening. In the middle of this lengthy reading, we hear again a despairing parent who has difficulty reaching his
children, who begs them to do right in the world: "'Learn to do good…
Come let us reach an understanding,' says the Lord" (1:17–18). It is a plea
to negotiate the terms of the relationship. For even when a family is in
crisis, there must surely be some shared values, some shared language,
with which to reach out across the abyss. As parents, we search for this
language all of the time.

Isaiah presents the difficult side of parenting through the inner landscape of our Divine Parent. Children in the abstract are the things of fairytales and magical worlds, objects of cuteness and amusement, precious angels who bring us only pride and joy. But this myth of children can be a source of terrible guilt for parents when they are elbow-deep in dishwater, amidst the drudgery of laundry, and managing a temper tantrum on the side. Every once in a while, you will hear a young mother confess: "No one told me it was going to be this hard."

Many years ago, a lovely and naive student asked me if raising children was a spiritual activity for me. "Yes," I replied, "when they're sleeping." I did not mean this as a joke. Children are indeed beautiful, peaceful and angelic when they are sleeping. And when they're awake they can be very animate and demanding. We invest our physical strength and our soul in them, and, as God shares through the voice of Isaiah, they are not always attentive or grateful. We love and care for them nonetheless, and save our reservoirs of pride and delight to get us through the more challenging moments.

Yet another *haftara*, the second of the season, is from Jeremiah (2:4–28), and it touches on the same painful point. In sharp language, it details the mistakes of our ancestors that pulled them away from God, creating an immense separation. But the most painful metaphor is again that of parent and child in a relationship that is filled with grief. The *haftara* is long and tiring; we feel weighted by its dense language and criticism. By the time we get to the end, we are not prepared for the rabbinic inclusion of a surprise verse from the next chapter of Jeremiah: "Just now you called to Me, 'Father! You are the companion of my youth'" (Jeremiah 3:4). Instead of leaving us with a relationship gone sour, the *haftara* jumps elsewhere and leaves us with a glimpse of reconciliation.

There are several interpretations of this verse that offer insight about the parent-child relationship. Rashi reads it as a rhetorical lament: "If only you would call Me 'Father.'" God pines for the intimacy of father and son, but it is elusive. It escapes even God. The first three verses of the chapter are not included in the *haftara*, but help explain Rashi's reading. They speak of betrayal using yet another family metaphor, that of husband and wife. Jeremiah 3:3 reads: "And when showers were withheld and the late rains did not come, you had the brazenness of a street woman, you refused to be ashamed." When you were desperate for rain, you were willing to do anything, even compromise your sexual integrity by breaking the sacred bond of marriage and parading in the streets like a harlot. When there is no rain, we are supposed to cry out to God. Only then do we realize our limitations and realize how much is beyond our control. Instead, we turned away.

Other commentators are more generous. They see this call as the breaking point, a way back to repentance. In the midst of alienation, there is a sudden deep need for closeness, for intimacy, that forces out the word "father." The distance collapses in this one small word.

This is not the first time that the word "father" is used in this *haftara*. In 2:27, God claims that the Israelites worshiped idols using the same language of parenthood: "They said to wood, 'You are my father,' to stone, 'You gave birth to me,' while to Me they turned their backs and not their faces. But in their hour of calamity they cry, 'Arise, save us.'" The children of Israel turned their backs from their real Creator and prayed to inanimate objects as if they were parents, even though they could give them nothing in return.

The confusion of identity, of not knowing who is one's real father, is the underlying drive of the paternity suit. An abandoned child, longing to know the identity of his real father, thinks of every male as potentially filling that absent space.

As we read the words of Isaiah and Jeremiah, we see a picture of a family in turmoil. A father and his estranged adolescent son are arguing. The child wants more independence; he tries to break away and assert himself. The father feels scorned and used. Others have replaced him as the center of the child's universe; friends and acquaintances all seem more important than the very parent who gave him life. In the height of accusation and dissent, there is suddenly the meek voice of need: "Father!" The father turns in surprise. Did you call me father? Suddenly the father is taken back to another time and place, to the days when his young, innocent son held his hand and walked with him in the park. He remembers that he was once the "companion of [his child's] youth," his son's best friend and hero. All of this because of one word of love: father.

Only when we place ourselves squarely within the "conversation" of this verse do we feel its emotional expansiveness. "Just now you called to Me, 'Father! You are the companion of my youth.'" We feel the vulnerability and fragility of the father who is wishing away the distance separating him from his son, and the son who sometimes needs, even in independence, especially in times of rebellion, the strong and protective embrace and praise of his father. But this is not the story of one family; it is a metaphor of a nation, as it states in Malachi 2:10, "Have we not all one Father?"

Kavana for the Day

Think of a parent, family member or close friend who is estranged from you right now, either intentionally or because you've lost touch. Write down what your relationship once was and what you valued about that person. Consider what factors contributed to the change your relationship has undergone. Make contact. Don't wait. What did it feel like to rekindle that spark, even if only temporarily, with few expectations? What burdens, joys and complications are attached to that connection?

Day Five: 21 Tammuz

Growth through Discomfort

We grow only through discomfort. When we are comfortable, there's no reason to change. The book of Proverbs helps us appreciate the voices of those who make us feel uncomfortable with ourselves: "He who criticizes a man will in the end find more favor than he who flatters him" (Proverbs 28:23). We all love compliments. They make us feel special and connected to the person who offers them. But Proverbs tells us to be wary of the flatterer, the person who gives us too many compliments. We will do better with the person who offers us solid criticism that can help us grow and change in the future, than with one who offers us the fleeting luxury of a feel-good moment. How well do you take criticism? How well do you give it?

The book of Proverbs contains many descriptions of the wise man and the foolish one, comparing and contrasting them, praising one and criticizing the other. One of the most meaningful differences between the wise person and the fool is how they each take criticism. "Do not criticize the fool for he will hate you. Correct the wise man, and he will love you" (ibid. 9:8).

To understand why wisdom requires criticism, we have to think about the nature of rebuke. To do so, we turn to the very first verses of Deuteronomy, to the *parasha* of *Devarim*, the Torah portion that is always read during the Three Weeks. The Hebrew word "*devarim*" means "words" or "things." In fact, words *are* things, giving the translation double weight. Many will shrug off an abuse of language with the simple dismissal, "It's just words," but Jewish tradition, from its semantic roots, treats words as having the concreteness of objects. They are our intellectual and emotional currency; they exist in the world. They are not wind or air that circulates lightly among us. They have weight and measure. Selecting the right words, the right context in which to use those words, and the right people to whom to say them is the better part of wisdom, especially when it comes to giving criticism.

When it comes to the things that we have to say, but don't always want to say, we look to Moses for advice. We open the book of Words/ Things and read the following verses: "These are the words that Moses addressed to all Israel on the other side of the Jordan. Through the wilderness, in the Arabah, near Suph, between Paran and Tophel, Laban, Hazeroth, and Di-Zahab, it is eleven days from Horeb to Kadesh-Barnea by the Mount Seir route. It was in the fortieth year, on the first day of the eleventh month, that Moses addressed the Israelites..." (Deuteronomy 1:1–3). Rashi adds layers of nuance to what seems like a typical biblical introduction, merely offering us the place and time of events. Moses, he contends, gathered everyone together so that there was no one absent who could later say that Moses spoke and no one contended with him. In other words, when everyone is present at a speech and hears the same words, there can be argument over interpretation but no refutation. Everyone knows who spoke up in debate. Rashi cites this ancient midrashic reading because the verse says "to *all* Israel," an expression which is surprisingly rare in describing Moses' audience. The actual words, "See, you are all here; he who has anything to say in reply, let him reply," is a remarkably democratic position. If Moses is going to chastise the Israelites for a difficult past, let all be present to hear it so that anyone can counter, if anyone dares.

All of the complicated place names that may mean little to later readers are locations where the Israelites sinned. Rashi surmises that the audience would have well understood the significance – and implicit shame – in the mention of these specific stops along the way; the text does so subtly, Rashi observes, to protect the honor of the Israelites. While we may not be able to recall the import of these places, we can understand the significance that names embody. Consider how we can immediately conjure images of freedom just by naming a few cities: Gettysburg, Selma, Philadelphia, Boston, Jamestown.

Why does Moses gather everyone together in the last year of this wearying journey? Any number of possibilities come to mind. He could be preparing them for life in the Promised Land, giving over laws that they have not had to keep thus far, but that would be critical as they neared the land – such as laws related to war, to agriculture and to the formation of a government – all matters that are discussed in this last of the five books. He could review history and offer his perspective on the past, which is certainly one way that this farewell speech is understood. He could be preparing final words of inspiration, since he knows that he will not be making the last leg of the journey.

Rashi believes that Moses, following in the footsteps of Jacob, Joshua, Samuel and David, gathered everyone together to rebuke them before he took leave of this world. There is something harsh and grating in this idea, that the last words of a beloved and beleaguered leader to his followers are words of chastisement. The *Sifrei*, the midrashic compilation on Deuteronomy, presents four reasons why people offer rebuke on their deathbeds: in order to criticize once rather than repeatedly; the shame of the person criticized is mitigated by the fact that this is a final meeting; to prevent the person who is rebuked from harboring a grudge against the rebuker; in order that they may part in peace.

Each of these reasons aims at clearing a path so the relationship can move forward. The last words someone utters are profoundly impactful, and stay embedded in the receiver's mind, precisely because they are the last ones. If you were to hear criticism again and again it would wash over you without really making a soulful mark. Sincere and thoughtful feedback not only fulfills the biblical command, "You shall not hate your brother in your heart; you shall surely rebuke your friend" (Leviticus 19:7), it also helps clear the barriers that stand in the way of a relationship. Rather than a final parting with the mystery of words unsaid, a last-ditch effort at advice and guidance can be its own meaningful legacy, a gift from the person who is leaving us forever.

Although Maimonides tells us how best to give difficult feedback – softly, in private and for the good of the person and not for our own good (Laws of Character 6:7) – we all still struggle with hearing it well and not putting up our defenses. Rabbeinu Bahya ben Asher, the thirteenth-century Spanish scholar, writes in his introduction to Deuteronomy that Moses gathered everyone together to leave his ethical last will and testament, even though not all in the group were willing to listen:

> It is well known that most rebukes [sic] are directed at the average person, the masses; the masses have different views, are not homogeneous … Seeing that all these people do not have minds of their own, they do not easily accept rebukes [sic] seeing that what one person likes another dislikes. What is pleasing to one person is unacceptable to others.[1]

When in the presence of many people, it is always easy to believe that the rabbi offering up a heated sermon, or an angry boss at a staff meeting, is talking to or about someone else.

Rabbeinu Bahya quotes two Talmudic passages to validate his reading. One states that younger scholars are preferred over older ones because the younger scholars are less critical.[2] It's easier to be popular if you make people feel good than if you make people feel challenged. The other reflects the words of Rabbi Tarfon: "I wonder if there exists in this generation anyone who knows how to accept rebuke."[3]

The way that we give and receive criticism is often shaped by culture, community expectations and societal norms. When we are defensive, we lose a whole avenue to introspection that can help us develop and grow in our sensitivity and thoughtfulness to others. Think of the helpful words of a mentor, a supervisor, or someone who took your last

1. *Torah Commentary by Rabbi Bahya ben Asher*, trans. Eliyahu Munk, vol. 7 (Jerusalem: Lambda Publishers, G 48 1998), 2348.
2. *Ketubot* 105a.
3. *Erkhin* 16b.

performance review seriously and gave you feedback that might not have been comfortable to hear but helped you become a better professional. Or the friend who you thought insulted you, but actually helped you become a better parent. There's the word your wife said that offended you, but that made you see that you weren't treating one of your children with the proper respect. Every day we receive messages about ourselves. Every once in a while, someone cares enough to tell us what they see. Correct the wise person and he will love you...

Kavana for the Day

Part one: Ask someone who is close to you either professionally or personally for feedback about something very specific. Listen carefully and prompt with questions. Think afterwards about what they said, how it made you feel, and what you're going to do about it.

Part two: Think of a relationship that has suffered because you have not been telling someone what you really think. Find a way to give respectful feedback that shows love and concern. How did you do?

Day Six: 22 Tammuz

With God in the Garden

When we imagine being with God in the garden, our imaginations turn to the Garden of Eden, the ultimate garden. God planted the garden as a food source for animals and humans before the creation of humankind. No doubt, it was also a place of beauty and mystery, a place where Adam tried to hide from God but where God's Presence swept through the trees and found him. We, too, see God in nature, just as Adam did.

Adam and Eve were placed in the garden as its stewards "to work it and look after it" (Genesis 2:15). They were there to observe its changes and thereby appreciate the relationship between nature and the divine, and they were to cultivate it. Adam, from the Hebrew "*adama,*" earth, was created as a mixture of the breath of God and the dust of the earth. Human beings, from their ancient and sacred beginnings, were to be custodians of the land that birthed them and sustained them.

This mythic, primordial universe is evoked in a curious rule. According to Jewish law, we are not allowed to plant fruit trees during the nine days before Tisha B'Av. Why?

Fruit trees occupy a special place in biblical literature. Those who plant fruit trees in the land of Israel must wait a full three years before enjoying the fruit, and must mark the maturation of the tree by bringing its first fruits to the Temple in Jerusalem in the fourth year. The patience demanded of the planter has long-term rewards. Trees that invest energy in growing roots rather than developing fruit will have a deeper root system – a critical requisite for the tree's viability in the hot, dry climate of the Middle East. We can imagine the joy that those first pomegranates, grapes and figs must have brought to the ones who planted them. The act of sacrifice brings with it profound gratitude, and imbues the simple act of planting with sanctity.

Trees and their fruit are a vital source of food and nutrition, especially in a country beset by famine, as we learn from the account of Abraham's earliest days on the land. Making sure that these trees have their highest yield is a small but significant insurance policy against the ravages of drought and hunger. Protecting fruit trees is the focus of another Deuteronomic law, which demands that fruit trees not be destroyed during war. Trees were often chopped down on the battle-field, since enemies could hide behind them; a field cleared of trees made human targets more visible and vulnerable. But fruit trees were not to become another tool in the human war machine since they are a food source. It takes a long time for a fruit tree to reach its full maturity and a short time to destroy it; the Torah demands that we take this into consideration, even when it comes to our adversaries.

A famous Talmudic passage in Tractate *Ta'anit* describes an old man planting a tree, one that in his lifetime, he will never see in full bloom. He defends his action on the grounds that he is planting for those who come after him, an act of foresight. It is that foresight that Deuteronomy is protecting.

Fighting is temporal. Wars end. We may unfortunately have to defend ourselves against enemies, but that should not deprive our opponents of their food source, especially when wars end. A field whose fruit trees have been cut down because of war cannot provide sustenance and survival for its inhabitants in the future.

Because fruit trees are a source of happiness, and elemental to a life lived off the land, we are forbidden to experience the pure joy of planting them during the Three Weeks. In a *haftara* cited earlier (Jeremiah 2:4–28, 3:4), Jeremiah uses a metaphor of planting that opens up a world of botanical delight and terror. "I planted you with noble vines, all with choicest seed; alas, I find you changed into a base, an alien vine!" (2:21). The image of God as a gardener, gently placing a choice seed among very special plants, is a tender, loving image. The vine is a hardy plant that ascends and spreads itself. Thus, in Psalms 128:3, the happy man is described as having a wife who is "like a fruitful vine within your house." In Micah 4:4, the vine is again the symbol of the happy homesteader: "They shall sit every man under his vine and under his fig tree." God as biblical gardener is an image that appears in Exodus 15:17, in the Song of the Sea, where God promises to plant the Israelites on His own mountain, protected from any danger. It is also used in Psalms as a powerful image of resettlement:

> You plucked up a vine from Egypt; you expelled nations and planted it. You cleared a place for it; it took deep root and filled the land. The mountains were covered by its shade, mighty cedars by its boughs. Its branches reached the sea, its shoots to the river. (Psalms 80:9–12)

Here, the once-small vine takes root, overpowering mountains and the tall, majestic cedar tree. Its branches, like rivers on a map, extend to the sea.

Jeremiah's vine is not as stable as a cedar nor as thick as its trunk. The Israelites-as-vine image is one of historical resonance. Thin and spidery branches that reach out far beyond their root system are an apt description for Jews throughout their history in the Diaspora. Even as a small minority their influence was far-reaching.

In this reading, the vine that is Israel was planted with the greatest of care. But as it grew, it became a gardener's nightmare. It became a base and alien vine among other noble plantings. Not only did it morph into something unrecognizable to the planter, it also imperiled other plants nearby. Vigilant gardeners spot such plants and uproot them so that the damage they cause will not have permanent consequences. Weeds that grow quickly can squeeze out other shoots. Someone once defined weeds as anything you don't want in your garden. Even beautiful flowers can become weeds if they don't allow their neighboring plants to grow and flourish.

But God blessed Israel with power: "To uproot and to pull down, to destroy and to overthrow, to build and to plant" (Jeremiah 1:10). Although the verse begins with uprooting, it ends with building and planting – the enduring element of Israel-as-gardener.

A vine is generally a fast-growing plant that can spread its beauty far and wide. But it can also choke other life around it and become the base, alien plant that Jeremiah describes. We are challenged to plant with care and to watch over that which we plant so that our vines provide comfort and shade but avoid being destructive, insinuating themselves into every crevice and choking other life.

In the utopian garden that is the Land of Israel, Jeremiah promised a repentant Israel the admiration of its neighbors: "In sincerity, justice and righteousness, nations shall bless themselves by you and praise themselves by you." When the nation of Israel lives by its covenant with God, it will become a show garden; it will be lauded by those around it. It will be a place of beauty and pride.

Kavana for the Day

From Ecclesiastes to *Death of a Salesman*, planting a garden has always been an act of hope. Remember those early biology experiments we did in school where we planted a seed in a Styrofoam cup and waited impatiently for the seed to grow? There was a thrill when the fragile green shoot pushed through the dirt. Every bloom and blossom can communicate this thrill to the gardener who sees in each development the progress and renewal of life. Consequently, in addition to the prohibition of planting fruit trees for food, it is also forbidden to plant trees for shade or fragrance during the last nine days of the Three Week period. And yet, to communicate hope and redemption, think about planting a tree right after the Three Weeks – a "Jewish" tree that becomes your symbol of hope in the future.

Day Seven: 23 Tammuz
Consolations

According to Jewish law, there are four blessings that are made only once a year. One of them is made on Tisha B'Av and appears in the middle of the *Amida* prayer of the afternoon service.[1] It is there that we acknowledge something unique about this fast day, above and beyond all others. Every day, three times daily, we pray for the rebuilding of Jerusalem and the ingathering of exiles. Every fast day, we insert special additional pleadings to intensify our supplications. But only on this one day a year do we add a prayer for consolation.

At times of distress, we search for comfort, solace and empathy. When we feel low, we want companionship. We may not know – indeed, we rarely do – why this great anguish has come upon us. We cannot understand it. Consolation, when sincere, can help fill in the gaps of incomprehension. When we have warmth, comfort and company, our failure to figure out life's great mysteries somehow matters less.

A tale is told among Hasidim about a young man who had

---

1. The other three are the blessing over the candle-lighting on Yom Kippur, the blessing over the first fruits that appear in the Hebrew month of Nisan, and *bi'ur ḥametz*, the blessing recited when leaven products are burned before Pesaḥ.

suffered many great personal losses, and traveled far to see his rebbe, seeking clarity and renewed faith at a time that sorely tried him. He arrived at the rebbe's court and blurted out his catalogue of misfortunes. The rebbe sat in silence and listened. Even when this disciple had finished, the rebbe sat in a prolonged and pregnant silence. The young man trembled. Finally, the rebbe got up and stood right next to his disciple and said in a hushed tone, "I cannot explain why any of these terrible things have befallen you. But I can stand beside you in anger." That is consolation.

The special prayer of consolation we recite is a lengthy paragraph. Pay attention to its metaphors and the intricacies of its language:

> Console, O Lord our God, the mourners of Zion and the mourners of Jerusalem, and the city that is in sorrow, laid waste, scorned and desolate; that grieves for the loss of its children, that is laid waste of its dwellings, robbed of its glory, desolate without inhabitants. She sits with her head covered like a barren childless woman. Legions have devoured her; idolaters have taken possession of her; they have put Your people Israel to the sword and deliberately killed the devoted followers of the Most High. Therefore Zion weeps bitterly, and Jerusalem raises her voice. My heart, my heart grieves for those they killed; I am in anguish, I am in anguish for those they killed. For You, O Lord, consumed it with fire, and with fire You will rebuild it in the future, as is said, "And I Myself will be a wall of fire around it, says the Lord, and I will be its glory within" [Zechariah 2:9].
>
> Blessed are You, Lord, who consoles Zion and rebuilds Jerusalem.

This is a curious blessing. What kind of blessing offers a review of the tragic events that require consolation? Is it not odd that the prayer actually makes us feel worse before it makes us feel better? Jerusalem as a barren woman – as one who not only had children and lost them to exile, but as one who never had any children at all – bent over and disgraced, offers us the image of the woman alone in her suffering. She cries out, but no one is there to listen. Her insides bewail the losses all around her.

Her enemies have triumphed and carried a nation away from its spiritual center. Is this review meant to offer us comfort or make us grieve harder? The prayer is bookended with the image of God as consoler. God is introduced at the beginning of the blessing as the one who consoles mourners, as if He were going to the *shiva* house of the entire Jewish people. At its closing, God is described not as a comforter but as a protector, a fire-wall. This image comes from Zechariah 2:9, from a chapter of consolation spoken by the prophet who led the Israelites out of Babylon and back to Zion. Immediately preceding the verse chosen for our liturgy is a celebratory passage that stands in sharp contrast to Jerusalem as an abandoned city: "Jerusalem shall be peopled as a city without walls, so many shall be the people and cattle it contains" (Zechariah 2:8). The walls that contained the fires of devastation will be bursting with inhabitants. They will be knocked down to accommodate the flooding of people. The language is exhilarating:

> "Shout for joy, Zion! For Lo, I come, and I will dwell in your midst," declares the Lord. In that day, many nations will attach themselves to the Lord and become His people, and He will dwell in your midst. (Zechariah 2:14–15)

This is more than the consolation of comfort. It offers a picture of the future, and communicates hope and optimism. Zechariah's image makes us want to join in the momentum of redemption. He extends the appeal of Zion far beyond the nation alone. Everyone will want to be there. God will be a magnet to newcomers and will dwell in Zion. God's presence will be securely felt.

The contrast between our prayer and Zechariah's hopefulness raises the question of how to define consolation. Consolation is not meant to be a distraction. It is not about looking elsewhere, in the future, to the side, somewhere other than despair. Zechariah's visions are prophetic and futuristic. Consolation is about looking exceedingly closely at a past from which it is all too easy to turn away and deriving meaning and comfort from it. It is the confrontation of grief in company.

Think about a visit to a mourner, a house of *shiva*. Many mourners during the shiva period try to focus all conversation on the person lost. We are there to be together with the mourner as he looks back. The consolation is in the details, in the reflection and contemplation of a life and the often sad and heart-wrenching last months and days. One can only really get to the other side of tragedy by immersing oneself in it and then emerging. Doctors often recommend that mourners not take medications that numb anxiety or ease pain because it is well known that this failure to grieve intensely will only prolong an inability to move on.

Who truly provides consolation – those at a *shiva* who ignore the pain and speak of unrelated issues, or those who are not afraid to ask "When did your mother get sick?" "What did she have?" "How did you handle it?"? These questions do not minimize the pain; they invite the mourner into a dialogue about what really happened, into a human encounter more profound for its harsh honesty.

God consoles us in this prayer not by avoiding the pain but by mourning the loss with us. That is true empathy. We feel solace not when someone explains away the reason for our suffering or distracts us with images of a redeemed future, but when God stands beside us in our anger and disbelief.

Kavana for the Day

Who in your life needs consolation right now? Think of someone who, in the past year, lost a spouse, a parent, or a sibling. We know that the intensity of loss changes over time, but is never gone. Over the year, the mourner's experience is softened and cushioned. Most mourners are comforted by their respective communities during the *shiva* period, the initial seven days. Yet many people feel that the hardest point is when they get up from the *shiva* – when no one is in the house and suddenly the aloneness of the situation seems unbearable. Since the process of consolation takes time, call or get together with someone who has suffered a recent loss and ask them how they're doing. Don't just make it a quick question, show concentrated interest: how has life changed for you? How often do you think of the person you lost? What has brought you solace in these months? Some mourners may choose to be more private, but others may wish to be asked. Some may feel that people only really "cared" during the week of *shiva*. Mourning takes time. Consolation requires patience and extended compassion.

Day Eight: 24 Tammuz
Tarnished Gold

We can only imagine the horror of watching Jerusalem torn apart by its enemies, its buildings burning and its citizens ravaged. Witnesses to events see themselves as the eyes of history. They want future generations to feel the pain even without having seen the tragedy. It is a paradoxical challenge for us to mourn a past that we have never experienced. But, as creatures of history, the Jewish calendar calls upon us to relive such moments repeatedly.

Eikha offers us a glimpse from up close: "How is the gold become dim! How is the most fine gold changed! The hallowed stones are poured out at the top of every street" (Lam. 4:1). Every street corner of ancient Jerusalem was littered with the Temple's pieces, its sacred gems. The finest of golden instruments used in ritual worship had been debased. Their worth was dulled because they could no longer be used to worship God. They became vessels valued only for their weight in gold, losing their religious significance.

The language of *Eikha* is powerful. It brings to mind media images of floods and fires where charred personal items of value are piled together, a tangle of memory, lost history and beauty. We may recall the residues of large scale tragedies summed up in the remains of a decimated wedding album or a torn love letter, piles of old shoes or a stack of winter coats. We hold on to these sacred gems that are spilled at every street corner because they are the last remaining pieces of an era – a place and time told in scattered fragments.

The detritus of exile and destruction is largely unrecorded and unremembered. In the rush to save oneself or to escape, things get left behind – objects that have meaning when life is safe but cannot always be taken along when life gets difficult. Jewish immigrants left behind homes, clothing, heirlooms. Maybe, if they were lucky, they brought a sewing machine to their new port of call so that they had a professional start in their next landing. Libraries have been broken apart or buried when their owners were forced to leave. Artwork and items of value were stolen and carted away to decorate someone else's walls. Few Jews are lucky enough to have extensive family heirlooms because they simply couldn't take anything with them. The gems are scattered and the gold dulled, with no one to polish it. If objects could speak they might tell powerful stories of travel and loss.

And yet, as the chapter in *Eikha* continues, it seems to change direction. Instead of remaining in the material realm of objects, the objects come to symbolize the people: "The precious sons of Zion, comparable to fine gold, how are they esteemed as earthen pitchers, the work of the hands of the potter!" (ibid. 4:2). Suddenly, the text defines what gold truly is for us. The real gold is not in the buildings but in the builders, the precious children of Zion who were decimated, shattered like simple earthenware thrown to the ground. Their worth as human beings was no longer valued. They were broken, their shards scattered everywhere.

The leaders of the community are compared to rubies and sapphires. And yet they too are "not recognized in the streets" (ibid. 4:8). Rashi makes the comparison complete: "Sacred stones are the children whose faces shine like precious jewels."

Jewish history, like these open streets, is littered with the remains of buildings, objects and people no longer with us, the shining faces that we'll never see, the dulled gold that is displaced and then disappears. As memory holders, we are obligated to honor the memory of loss by making space for the emptiness.

Kavana for the Day

We think of ourselves as descendants but not always as ancestors. One day, far into the future, we will be ancestors to family members we will never know. What objects of ours will tell our Jewish story for them? If you have no Jewish heirlooms, now may be a time to buy some items of ritual significance. They don't need to be expensive; they just have to tell a piece of your narrative. And, in terms of ancestors, now is a great time to honor the memory of those no longer with us by either displaying special objects of the past, making a scrapbook, investigating your family tree with your children, or interviewing a family member. Make memory come alive. Be a witness. Tell your story.

Day Nine: 25 Tammuz

Never Abandon Zion

Each day in our prayers, we ask that our eyes should return to Zion, "*Vetehezena einenu beshuvekha leTziyon.*" It is not only about being in Israel in body – it is also about a focus towards Israel, an enduring, directed vision. No matter what our eyes look at, they should return their gaze to Zion. When we contemporize these ancient sentiments, we think about what it means for us to direct our hearts and souls to Zion at a time of rampant, global delegitimization of the State of Israel. In the words of Gil Troy in his book, *Why I Am a Zionist*:

> I am a Zionist because I am an idealist, and just a century ago, the notion of a strong, independent, viable, sovereign Jewish state was an impossible dream – yet absolutely worth fighting for – so, too, today, the notion of a strong, independent, viable, sovereign state living in true peace and harmony with its neighbors appears to be an impossible dream – yet absolutely worth striving for.[1]

---

1. Gil Troy, *Why I am a Zionist* (Montreal: Bronfman Jewish Education Centre, 2006), p. 3.

The Three Weeks is a good time for each of us to consider the relationship we have with Israel, not as a political entity or a tourist site, but as Zion, the biblical name that signifies the unique spiritual homeland. Many of the travails bemoaned by the prophets that are read in the Three Weeks point to the growing abyss between the dream of Zion and the dystopia that has evolved because those living in Zion have lost their moral compass.

Open to virtually any page of *Eikha* and you will encounter the image of a beautiful Zion laid bare. "How has the Lord covered the daughter of Zion with a cloud in His anger, and cast down from heaven to earth the beauty of Israel" (Lam. 2:1). Zion is compared to a mother bereft of children, a maid walking aimlessly in the streets, a woman vulnerable to hostilities. Imagining Zion as a woman is a way to trigger compassion. "How does the city sit solitary, that was full of people! How is she become like a widow, she that was great among the nations" (ibid. 1:1).

One particularly painful image is that of the lonely and isolated Zion described in the first chapter of Isaiah – which is one of the *haftarot* read during these weeks:

> And the daughter of Zion is left like a shelter in a vineyard, like a lodge in a garden of cucumbers, like a besieged city. If the Lord of hosts had not left us a very small remnant, we should have been like Sodom, and we should have been like Gomorrah. (Isaiah 1:8–9)

That Sodom and Gomorrah are mentioned here as examples of places that have lost their way is not surprising. The story of these immoral cities is told in Genesis 19 as a cautionary tale of what happens to an area steeped in illicit behavior. Throughout the Bible, these cities are held up as paradigms of poor real estate choices. Wicked neighbors have influence. To illustrate, in Deuteronomy 29:22, we read: "The whole land is brimstone, and salt, and burning, that it is not sown, nor bears, nor does any grass grow on it, like the overthrow of Sodom and Gomorrah." Cities that are barren of those of good deeds are locations to avoid. Isaiah states that Zion has not yet reached that point but is on its way. There are still some surviving people of integrity, but Zion is becoming like these places of ill-repute.

Then the prophet uses a confusing image: Zion is a booth in both a vineyard and a cucumber patch. Not being farmers, most modern readers will be perplexed by this comparison. Sodom and Gomorrah is understandable; a cucumber garden seems a little too tame for what the prophet is trying to achieve with his language.

If we were readers from the past living in an agrarian society, the image would be immediately meaningful. Booths were placed in vineyards and fields that were usually far away from the owner's home. At the time of harvest, predators and thieves would often steal crops. Booths were places where farm hands and workers could seek refuge from the hot Middle Eastern sun and were a base for guards posted to scare away animals or potential thieves.

A booth standing empty in an uncultivated field is a sign of loss and alienation. It means that there is no one to protect the field or vineyard. It means that a place of growth and productivity is lying in waste and desolation. This meaning is backed up by the reference to Sodom and Gomorrah. These cities are not mentioned because of what happened in them; they are mentioned because after they burned down, their remains laid empty and desolate with no signs of renewal. These cities became places with no human habitation or protection.

When we think of Zion, we think of a place flourishing with an ideology, its inhabitants driven by a mission. That homeland, the prophet says, should never be abandoned and desolate. It is our job to protect it. This ancient message for the farmer is just as relevant for us today. We cannot abandon Zion at this time. It cannot stand alone in the world of nations but must be protected, embraced and supported in every way. Martin Buber once wrote powerfully of the ancient vision of our prophets:

> The renewal of the world and the renewal of Zion are one and the same thing, for Zion is the heart of the renewed world...The people of Israel is called upon to be the herald and pioneer of

the redeemed world, the land of Israel to be its center and the throne of its King."[2]

Kavana for the Day

There are so many ways to connect to Israel. We can eat Israeli food, call a friend or relative who lives there, buy Israeli music or read a novel in translation. These small bridges mean a lot when we think of them within the larger framework of not "abandoning Zion."

When is the last time you did something to support Israel? It may be an action that ranges from visiting Israel when tourism is down, to supporting an Israeli charity, or writing a letter to someone in Congress when Israel is isolated in the world or to a newspaper when it is getting bad press. The delegitimization of Israel is one of the great challenges of our age and this is an important season to ask ourselves if we are truly well-informed advocates for the Jewish state. We are blessed to have autonomy and independence, a place of pride and refuge for Jews the world over, for the first time in two thousand years. What are you doing to celebrate Israel?

2.   Martin Buber, *On Zion* (New York: Schocken Books, 1973), p. 35.

Day Ten: 26 Tammuz

The Divine Romance

Maimonides, in trying to explain the love of a human for God, compared the relationship to the romance between a man and a woman.[1] The desire, the flirtation, the temptation and the passion can all be translated into the context of the divine. This explains traditional readings of *Shir HaShirim*, the Song of Songs, as a sustained metaphor for the love between God and humanity played out as a human romance in the orchards and spice hills of Israel. Carrying the comparison further, we consider the pain of heartbreak, the anguish of a woman scorned or a man left alone after a longstanding relationship. The investment is wasted, the love thins and the pain scars. God plays this out with the Israelites, too, when they betray their romance with their ultimate Partner.

One such romantic break-up took place when Jerusalem went into exile during the reign of King Jehoiakim, the son of King Josiah. Jehoiakim was a ruthless king, immune to Jeremiah's words of warning. He shredded Jeremiah's scroll of chastisement with a knife and threw its predictions into the fire. Jeremiah then prepared the Israelites for the exilic consciousness of life outside the Holy Land.

---

1. Maimonides, *Mishneh Torah*, "Laws of Repentance" 10:3.

In the third chapter of Jeremiah – another one of the *haftarot* read in these weeks – we find the comparison of Israel's idolatry to adultery. One of the greatest unspoken fears we have in love and marriage is that of betrayal. We age, and we worry that perhaps we are not as attractive or as interesting as we once were. If the marriage grows stale, will he look elsewhere? Will she find real happiness with someone else? Anxiety about rejection looms large in the dark chambers of the heart.

The Israelites' lack of faithfulness is contrasted to God's everlasting hope that they will one day return. The rebellious Israelites are an adulterous wife. This comparison not only created a literary mirror through which Israel could view its actions, it was also a metaphoric way to communicate God's loss.

> [The word of the Lord came to me] as follows: If a man divorces his wife, and she leaves him and marries another man, can he ever go back to her? Would not such a land be defiled? Now you have been with many lovers; can you return to Me? – says the Lord. (Jeremiah 3:1)

It is a simple and earnest question and one filled with grief. It takes two to make a relationship. What happens to trust when one partner is untrue but then wants to return to the marriage? Is trust possible?

The husband in this metaphor wants an exclusive relationship with his wife. He longs for the kind of intimacy that can only come with trust, but cannot be sure of his wife's fickle behavior. "I thought: After she has done all these things, she will come back to Me. But she did not come back..." (ibid. 3:7). Our heart goes out to this man. He is so desperate for his wife's love that despite her lies and betrayals, he is willing to take her back. We the readers do not believe she is worth it. But our judgments aside, she does not return to him anyway.

In Malachi, the tears of women whose husbands took other wives are absorbed into the altar of the second *Beit HaMikdash*: "The Lord is a witness between you and the wife of your youth with whom you have broken faith, though she is your partner and covenanted spouse...let no one break faith with the wife of his youth" (Malachi 2:14–15). Relationships should grow and intensify over time. Be wary of those who invite new partners into their lives and dismiss the devoted spouses of their younger days.

Martin Buber wrote in *I and Thou*, "Every real relation with a being or life in the world is exclusive...is single and confronts you. It fills the heavens. This does not mean that nothing else exists; but all else lives in its light."[2] This beautiful image of a relationship as a lens through which we view all else is expanded by Rabbi Louis Jacobs in *Jewish Thought Today*: "In every I–Thou relationship there is the special intimate meeting with another that makes everything else peripheral to the person encountered for as long as the relationship lasts."[3]

Buber speaks of intimacy. Beyond simple affection or emotional closeness, the relationship Buber points to is one of such profound attachment that life is almost continually seen through the lens of another. When a relationship reaches this level of intimacy, it does not mean that nothing exists but love or that there is total self-abnegation, but that all "lives in its light": everything is colored by the love for another human being. It is a powerful and animating force that gives people their very reason for living.

We find the intensity of the love described by Buber hinted at in a chapter earlier on in Jeremiah, in specific reference to the relationship between human and God at its peak: "Thus said the Lord: I accounted to your favor the devotion of your youth, your love as a bride – how you followed Me into the wilderness, in a land not sown" (Jeremiah 2:2). In love, we are willing to risk all and enter a universe of uncertainty, a wilderness that brings us no fear because we live in partnership. We are not alone.

Yet love can change from this kind of co-dependency to anger, resentment and loss when one partner betrays the other. The unit that we thought of as one was not one at all. People who suffer the unexpected infidelity of a partner feel that more than trust has been violated. Their knowledge of the world, their beliefs and assumptions, are profoundly shaken. "But I thought I knew her." Once these foundations begin to shake, the whole world seems to totter. "Perhaps every relationship that I have is not what it seems." Rather than blame the other, there is self-recrimination. "How could I not know?" "What did I do wrong?" We hear this reflected in God's words through the prophet: "I thought: After she has done all these things, she will come back to Me. But she did not come back..." (ibid. 3:7).

Rabbi Jonathan Sacks, writing about relationships and the notion of covenant, observes that,

> The great covenantal relationships – between God and mankind, between man and woman in marriage, between members of a community or citizens in a society – exist because both parties recognize that "it is not good for man to be alone." God cannot redeem the world without human participation; humanity cannot redeem the world without recognition of the divine.[4]

In true love, not only are we willing to risk all for an uncertain future, we are willing to forego our own emotional protection to take back that which is temporarily lost. In that rawness of vulnerability, we test the limits of compassion. As does God.

Kavana for the Day

This season of Jewish tragedy and betrayal is a time to review and renew flagging relationships. If you are in a marriage, list the three things you can do right now to strengthen intimacy. No matter how long you have been married or how well you know each other, you can still find ways to enhance trust, share kindnesses and offer unexpected love. We repair what is broken with enduring love and trust.

---

4. Rabbi Jonathan Sacks, *The Dignity of Difference* (London: Continuum, 2002), p. 203.

Day Eleven: 27 Tammuz

Answer Us

Who impedes me,
Why can't I disclose in writing all my thoughts,
The most hidden musings of my soul?[1]

These words, the opening of Rabbi Abraham Isaac HaKohen Kook's poem "Who Impedes Me?," offer a glimpse of man's spiritual vulnerabilities, vulnerabilities found even in so great a Jewish thinker and mystic. We search for language to reach across the abyss towards God, but so often come up short.

On fast days, we add special *tefillot* to our regular service to help us cross the abyss, to set the day apart and create a mood of supplication, of withdrawal from the universe of prosaic concerns. Prayer, Rabbi A.J. Heschel once wrote, "is an act consisting of a moment of decision or turning and of a moment of direction."[2] On every fast day, we make a

1. Rabbi Abraham Isaac HaKohen Kook, "Who Impedes Me?" in *Abraham Isaac Kook: The Lights of Penitence, The Moral Principles, Lights of Holiness, Essays, Letters, and Poems* (Mahwah, NJ: Paulist Press, 1978), p. 385.
2. Rabbi A.J. Heschel, *The Prophets*, Vol. II (New York: Harper, 1962), p. 220.

"turn" with a special plea, *"Anenu,"* inserted during Minḥa, the afternoon service, in the *"Shema Kolenu"* blessing of the Amida. In *Shema Kolenu* we pray, ironically, that God listen to our prayers. For all the desires and wishes we utter, our most fervent is that God hear us.

According to Jewish law, this special supplication should be said only by someone who is fasting, because the words combine with the act to create a posture of contrition before God. The *"Anenu"* prayer echoes the plea for God to listen to us, but heightens it with another demand: answer us. It sounds like hutzpah to demand God's ear and response, but we do it nonetheless. In the book of Lamentations, Jeremiah asked an irreverent question multiple times: *Eikha*, why? Had the prophet not asked it, we could not, because we believe in *tzidduk hadin*, in accepting the justice of our fate, even when we fail to understand it. We do so without question. But Jeremiah did question. He wanted God to explain the destruction of our beautiful city Jerusalem and the stripping of Zion and the anguish of mothers who lost their children. Why? What could justify this? In his memory, we use the same words. We ask God to explain.

The request to be answered may, in some ways, be more powerful than the questions we often ask in the face of tragedy, precisely because "why" can be asked as a rhetorical question of mystery, without expectation of an answer. In *Anenu* we put God on the spot:

> Answer us, Lord, answer us on our Fast Day, for we are in great distress. Look not at our wickedness. Do not hide Your face from us and do not ignore our plea. Be near to our cry; please let Your loving-kindness comfort us. Even before we call to You, answer us…

Whereas we normally ask God to listen, we now redouble our efforts and entreat God in multiple and different ways, hoping that something will be heard, hoping that God will respond.

On Tisha B'Av specifically, we add another special supplication in our Amida, a passage recited only once a year, also during the afternoon service: *Naḥem*, "console us." Listen, answer, console. We add this not in our personal petitions, but in the blessing that speaks of the rebuilding of Jerusalem, focusing our pain:

Console, O Lord our God, the mourners of Zion and the mourners of Jerusalem, and the city that is in sorrow, laid waste, scorned and desolate; that grieves for the loss of its children, that is laid waste of its dwellings, robbed of its glory, desolate without inhabitants.

If a person forgets to say this prayer at the correct place, it can be said later during *"Shema Kolenu,"* the blessing which offers a place to insert personal supplications. In other words, this clause said only once a year should not be bypassed if at all possible. We want people to articulate the specific loss of Jerusalem on Tisha B'Av, and we need God to offer us solace.

To return to *Anenu*, we ask that God answer us with kindness *before* we pray. What kind of request is this?

It is always more of a consolation if people understand our pain and reach out to us before we have to articulate our distress. We feel more loved when others can anticipate our feelings rather than when we have to spell them out. It makes us feel like we are the objects of their genuine concern. They have been thinking of us before we even told them of our distress. We find a powerful example of this in the book of Ruth. Ruth lost a husband and then made a choice to leave her homeland, her family and life as she knew it to journey with her mother-in-law to a strange land. Even after she had made an enormous commitment to become Jewish and accept Naomi's faith, God and people, Ruth is treated as an alien in Bethlehem. She is called the Moabite, a flashback to the life she willingly left. Only Boaz reaches out to her, and acknowledges her commitment:

It has been fully related to me, all that you have done for your mother-in-law since the death of your husband: and how you left your father and your mother, and the land of your birth, and went to a people whom you had not known before. May the Lord recompense your deed, and may a full reward be given to you by the Lord God of Israel, under whose wings you have come to take refuge. (Ruth, 2:11–12)

Boaz emphasizes that *God* will reward Ruth, even if others do not. He tries to minimize her suffering and alienation at the hands of human beings. God is all-knowing, and God can see beyond petty pigeonholing and labeling. Ruth answers Boaz's initial kindness with the words, "Why are you so kind to single me out when I am a foreigner?" (ibid. 2:10), and she repeats this theme with a variation: "You are most kind to comfort me and to speak gently to your maidservant – though I am not so much as one of your maidservants" (ibid. 2:13). Ruth had suffered so much isolation that she did not even see herself as worthy of kindness. But when Boaz noticed her, she found the strength to notice herself. When someone acknowledges our distress, we grow stronger through compassion and feel more empowered to confront our suffering. We find a voice.

In *Anenu* we ask God for kindness as a form of consolation. True kindness is when God reaches out to us before we express pain. Please let Your kindness comfort us, before we call You to answer us…

Kavana for the Day

Anenu prompts us to ask questions that force God to answer, initially focusing on our heartache but then transforming us into problem-solving beings. We fix whatever is broken from the place of our vulnerability. Our brokenness gives us a window into the brokenness of others. John F. Kennedy, in an address to the Irish Parliament, said, "The supreme reality of our time is our indivisibility as children of God and the common vulnerability of this planet."[3] The book of Psalms tells us that the whole world is built on loving-kindness (89:3). Everything is held in place by the glue of small interactions of goodness, of kindness to strangers at the time of their vulnerability. Today do one small act of kindness for someone you don't know. Help hold up our fragile world.

3. John F. Kennedy, speech to a joint session of the Dáil and the Seanad, Dublin, Ireland (*28 June 1963*).

Day Twelve: 28 Tammuz

Teaching God to Cry

O urs is an age which has forgotten how to cry." Rabbi Norman Lamm, chancellor of Yeshiva University, offered this observation in a sermon he gave on Rosh HaShana called "Three Who Cried."[1] Rosh HaShana is a time when many of us cry over ourselves and our wrongs, and sometimes over the state of the world. Rabbi Lamm speaks of three types of tears: the tears that come when our myths of absolute security and certainty are shattered; the tears of those who resign themselves to hopelessness; and the tears of those who cry over reality, not from frustration or resignation, but from a determination to change and renew that reality. Jewish crying fits the last of these categories: the act of crying, according to Rabbi Lamm, is the beginning of transformation – the tears are those of protest and resolute purpose.

But Rosh HaShana is not the only crying time of the year where we have perhaps forgotten the meaning and the power of tears. *Eikha* returns to the motif of crying again and again. We can visualize Jeremiah,

---

1. Norman Lamm, "Three Who Cried," speech given at the Jewish Center (New York City) on the first day of Rosh HaShana, September 29, 1962.

its attributed author, weeping ceaselessly as he writes. He tells us as much:

> My eyes are spent with tears, my heart is in tumult; my being melts away over the ruin of my poor people. (Lam. 2:11)

> When I cry and plead, He shuts out my prayer. (Ibid. 3:8)

> My eyes shed streams of water over the ruin of my poor people. (Ibid. 3:48)

> My eyes shall flow without cease, without respite until the Lord looks down and beholds from heaven. (Ibid. 3:49)

> Do not shut your ear to my groan, my cry. (Ibid. 3:56)

We hear a familiar refrain in Jeremiah's words: God is ignoring our tears. We sense multiple levels of pain in these verses. There is the anguish of destruction which prompts tears and then there is the additional weeping that occurs when God ignores the tears. Perhaps there is no pain greater than ignored pain. Just watch a child fall in a playground. The child in pain looks up to see if a parent is watching. With no parent to watch, he holds back the tears and continues to play. But when he sees that his mother is indeed watching, he bursts into tears, waiting for a nurturing embrace and someone to brush them away. Tears are one of the most powerful, wordless ways we communicate our feelings to others. To know that someone hears those tears and ignores them adds an additional element of suffering: "Do not shut your ear to my groan, my cry."

But what about God's tears? Does God ever cry about us? Do we ever ignore His cries? In the opening to *Eikha Raba*, an ancient rabbinic commentary on the book of Lamentations, there is an interpretation of the verse, "And God, the Lord of Hosts, called the day for crying and eulogizing" (Proem/*Petiḥta* 24). When our enemies broke into the *Mikdash* and conquered it, God said, "I no longer have a place in this world and will remove My Presence from it, back to its original resting place." And at that same time, God cried and said, "What have I done?

I placed My Divine Presence in the lower world for the sake of Israel and now that they have sinned, I have returned to My original dwelling." In the midrash, God then goes with the ministering angels to see the destruction of the *Mikdash* from up close, and He cries again, "Woe is Me over My House. My children, where are you? My priests, where are you? My loved ones, where are you?"

At this point, God speaks to Jeremiah of what He is experiencing. "Today I am like a man who made his only son a wedding canopy, and he died in the middle of the ceremony." God then tells Jeremiah to go and call upon his ancestors Abraham, Isaac, Jacob and Moses at their burial places since "they know how to cry." Jeremiah says that he does not know where Moses is buried (since we are told in Deuteronomy 34:6 that no one knows the location of Moses' grave). God tells him to go to the edge of the Jordan River and call out "Son of Amram, son of Amram." Jeremiah does this and asks Moses to petition God on behalf of Israel.

Moses asks Jeremiah why, but Jeremiah does not know (this midrash positions Jeremiah before the destruction. Here, the prophet has been denied the power to see the future). Moses then asks one of the ministering angels whom he knew from the time of Sinai to explain Jeremiah's request and is told of the upcoming destruction: "The Temple has been destroyed and Israel has been exiled." At that moment Moses begins to cry and petition so that his tears wake the patriarchs, and the angels rend their garments, put their hands on their heads, and scream and cry so that their tears reach the gates of the Temple. When God sees this spectacle, He declares a day of mourning.

This midrash explains the etiology of Tisha B'Av in an imaginative rendering of how tears prompted God to declare a day of mourning – and also describes how Jeremiah had to learn how to cry. He needed to take lessons from a master, Moses. And Moses needed the angels to cry with him so that the tears would reach the Temple. Finally, looking at all of this emotional unraveling, God Himself was also moved to tears.

Tisha B'Av is Jewish crying-time. It is a day when we look back at persecution and shed tears over the mess. Once a year we have to revisit a painful past where persecutions meld and merge into a continuous timeline of tragedy. We fast. We pray. We think. We cry.

What if we have forgotten how to cry? Though we may feel like crying, we so often hold back tears. Rabbi Lamm reflects on this in relation to Rosh HaShana, but his words are easily transferable to Tisha B'Av:

> Once upon a time the Maḥzor [High Holy Day prayer-book] was stained with tears; today it is so white and clean – and cold. Not, unfortunately, that there is nothing to cry about... It is rather that we have embarrassed ourselves into silence... And so the unwept tears and unexpressed emotions and the unarticulated cries well up within us and seek release. What insight the Kotzker Rebbe had when he said that when a man needs to cry, and wants to cry, but cannot cry – that is the most heart-rending cry of all.[2]

For us to feel the impact of the Three Weeks deeply, we have to allow ourselves the full range of sadness: grief, loss, remorse, guilt and confusion. We don't have to teach ourselves to cry. We just have to give ourselves permission.

Kavana for the Day

Has there ever been a time when you cried over the Jewish people? Think of that moment and what prompted it. What was the trigger that pushed you over the invisible emotional boundary line? Open up the book of *Eikha* and skim its verses. Identify the one that pains you the most. On Tisha B'Av, go back to that verse and read it several times until you feel that you have taken it in fully.

If you cannot cry over it, but want to learn how to cry, think of someone you could turn to in order to learn how to cry. What prompted that choice of person? What makes some people "good criers" and others less able to express emotion fully? When we give ourselves permission to cry and to experience the full range of pain that Jeremiah expresses, we also learn how to experience the intensity of joy.

2.   Ibid. See previous footnote.

Day Thirteen: 29 Tammuz

An Echo in the Ruins

What does it mean to pray on location? One of our ancient sages, Rabbi Yose, shares a fascinating observation on praying in the ruins of Jerusalem in the vicinity of Elijah the Prophet:

> Rabbi Yose said: "I was once traveling on a road, and I stopped in one of the ruins of Jerusalem to pray. Elijah, may he be remembered for goodness, came and guarded the door until I completed my prayers. When I finished...he said to me, "My son, why did you go into a ruin?"
>
> I responded: "To pray." [...]
>
> He said, 'What sound did you hear in the ruin?"
>
> I answered: "I heard a heavenly voice that cooed longingly like a dove and said, 'Woe to the children whose sins caused Me to destroy My Temple...then banish them among the nations.'"[1]

There is something compelling about praying near ruins. It focuses our prayer on what is and on what is no longer. It helps us appreciate our

---

1. *Berakhot* 3a

own safety and our history, as anyone who has prayed at the Kotel, the Western Wall, can attest. Rabbi Yose adds a more mystic dimension: he offers us the voices we hear from the past that resonate throughout buildings that are no longer in existence, the spiritual ghosts that we can hear but cannot see. Through those voices we imagine conversations that could have taken place.

Rabbi Yose creates a powerful dialogue, first with Elijah and then with God, the two voices he heard. Elijah guards the ruins because they may not have been a safe place to pray. In fact, in the Talmudic passage the prophet admonishes him not to pray in ruins but rather to pray on the road. Rabbi Yose retorts that he did not want to be interrupted, and so stepped into the ruins. Elijah then says he ought to have prayed more quickly, using a shorter version. But as they move beyond practical concerns, Elijah explores the experience more fully and wants to know what lies in the shadows of what once existed and is no more.

This allegorical conversation takes place after the destruction of the Second Temple. We have another set of voices after the destruction of the First Temple: Jeremiah's ruminations on what he saw in the ruins of Jerusalem. He finds another voice in the ruins.

> Gone is the joy of our hearts;
> Our dancing is turned into mourning.
> The crown has fallen from our head;
> Woe to us that we have sinned. (Lam. 5:15–16)

Eikha is a short biblical book of only five chapters whose poetic words are read with a melancholy musical notation. The minor-key melody creates a sense of the fragility of buildings and of human life. The tune offers us another voice that vibrates in the broken walls of memory. We close our eyes and imagine ashes fluttering in the fires over Jerusalem, and sense the isolation and despair of the prophet.

Towards the end of the elegy quoted above, Jeremiah turns away from the city towards a more obscure place: the human heart. Joy has dissipated. Happy activity has been replaced with grief. And the pride in Jerusalem, symbolized by the crown that offered us sparkle and height, has fallen to the floor. The image of a fallen crown is startling. We can think for a moment of prized royal jewels or anything of immense value that is treasured and cared for suddenly falling onto the floor, dismissed and useless, neglected and worthless.

Jeremiah creates for us a rich visual picture of the streets of Zion: the beggars and castoffs who are our ancestors and the crying, the endless crying that is the only real response when words fail us. Jeremiah is not only referencing a city. He is mourning the state of exile and the dislocation of those who are hated by the world. He takes us to a time when Jews were reviled and violently mistreated. Sadly, we do not have to go back as far as Jeremiah's days to understand his heavy-hearted sentiment.

Rabbi Yose and Jeremiah before him offer us the voice and melody of suffering. They hear the echoes of a lamentable past and help it find a haunting place within us.

Kavana for the Day

Spend a few moments writing a fictional dialogue about suffering. Include God and any figure from the Bible. It need not be long; some of the most potent dialogues are only a few words. Imagine yourself as Moses, Jeremiah, Job or Isaiah crying out to God. What is the conversation?

Day Fourteen: 1 Av

ROSH ḤODESH AV

Looking Forward, Looking Back

The Shabbat immediately before Tisha B'Av is referred to as "*Shabbat Ḥazon.*" A "*ḥazon*" is a vision or prophecy. Usually when we speak of visions we think optimistically about the future. The texts we recall on *Shabbat Ḥazon*, however, are of doom and devastation. The ancient Israelites are referred to as a brood of evildoers, as depraved children. God bemoans the loss of intimacy between Him and the people.

In this single chapter the destruction of Zion and Jerusalem is predicted. Sodom and Gomorrah are mentioned repeatedly; the sense of sin and the difficulty of extricating oneself from it weigh heavily on the reader. But one underlying theme emerges about the nature of the sin that brings about alienation from God: religious piety in place of human justice and equity. God criticizes the bringing of offerings to the Temple, and Holiday times filled with hypocrisy:

> Bring no more vain offerings; incense of abomination they are
> to Me; as for new moons and sabbaths and the calling of assem-
> blies, I cannot bear iniquity along with solemn meeting. Your
> new moons and your appointed feasts My soul hates: they are
> a trouble to Me; I am weary of enduring them. (Isaiah 1:13–14)

God articulates disgust through the agency of the prophet. Occasions
that are traditionally joyous have become burdensome. Why?

The reason for God's anger is mentioned twice in this chapter:
the neglect of widows and orphans. God remands the people: "Devote
yourself to justice; aid the wronged. Uphold the rights of the orphan;
defend the cause of the widow" (ibid. 1:17). This strong recommen-
dation is backed up by the reality that greed has blinded people from
helping those most vulnerable: "Your rulers are rogues and cronies of
thieves, every one avid for presents and greedy for gifts; they do not
judge the case of the orphans, and the widow's cause never reaches
them" (ibid. 1:23).

Neglect of widows and orphans is not a new theme in the biblical text. We are admonished in Exodus and Deuteronomy to care for
those most vulnerable in our society. What do Isaiah's strong words add?
Isaiah's point is a legal one. According to Rashi, the prophet is pointing
a finger at a justice system where bribes are accepted out of avarice, and
those unable to pay – like the widow and orphan – have their cases post-
poned to a later date. Because the vulnerable are not given top priority
in the justice system, they stop using the courts. Now we understand
the causative relationship in the verse: "They do not judge the case of
the orphans, and the widow's cause never reaches them." Because the
case of orphans is neglected, the widows never bother to come.

An indictment of a legal system is ultimately an indictment of
society. We all have moments when we ignore the urgent needs of
those around us. We don't do it willfully; we assume that *someone else*
will take care of the problem. Growing up in a democracy, we naturally
assume that when agreement cannot be reached between people, a
government agency will step in and adjudicate. Our tax payers' dollars
will come through; a social service institution or charitable non-profit
will pick up the pieces.

In the *haftara* for *Shabbat Ḥazon*, the prophet Isaiah presents a subtle message about the status of orphans and widows. We must ensure that they get the same legal protections and benefits as everyone else so that they, too, will experience the heft of justice and of an equitable system of law that offers them a fair hearing and a platform for grievance: "Uphold the rights of the orphan; defend the cause of the widow." Do not call yourself a pious person unless you are part of building a just society. "Though you pray at length," God says, "I will not listen" (ibid. 1:15). Those who cannot speak kindness and justice cannot be heard in their time of need. There is a language barrier. God will not hear the prayer of those who separate religious obligation from human compassion. The religious world view must encompass both.

Every day presents an opportunity to make our lives more whole, less fragmented, more honest and less compartmentalized. We are all hypocrites in one way or another. We strive to be good but stumble. We aim for consistency but miss the mark. So instead of trying to change the whole world at once, perhaps we can make minute but meaningful steps to promote justice. Small acts of justice are the bricks of any future *Mikdash*.

Kavana for the Day

According to the Talmud (*Shabbat* 31a), when we reach heaven at the end of our lives, God asks us a series of questions. One of them is: Have you worked for the world's redemption? This doesn't mean, "did you wait for the Messiah"; it implies that we must actively create the kind of environment where a messiah could exist and flourish, a place endowed with a spirit of compassion and social justice. There is no better way to redeem the neglect of the widow and orphan than by lending a hand towards the most vulnerable in society. Call up a local shelter and volunteer for a few hours. When we call it a shelter, we mean that it is a safe refuge for those who need temporary housing and protection. But ironically, we are often sheltered from the rawness of those who need its services because we live such cushioned lives. The shelter protects them, but distances us. "Un-shelter" yourself by seeing the way the other half lives. It may become a good habit.

Day Fifteen: 2 Av

Reversal of Fortune

After years of longing and praying, the barren Hannah finally has a son, on loan from God. He grows into the prophet Samuel. When she comes to the *Mishkan* to pay homage to God for this gift, she does not offer a prayer of thanksgiving. Instead, she waxes lyrical on the reversal of fortune:

> The bows of the mighty are broken,
> And the faltering are girded with strength.
> Men once sated must hire out for bread;
> Men once hungry hunger no more.
> While the barren woman bears seven,
> The mother of many is forlorn...
> The Lord makes poor and makes rich;
> He casts down, he also lifts high... (1 Samuel 2:4–7)

From a theological point of view, Hannah's observations about life may be more powerful than gratitude. She declares that life as we know it can change in an instant, as did hers. This provides more than thanks – it offers hope. It also forces humility on those who have been given much.

It can all be taken away *keheref ayin,* in the blink of an eye. The novelist Joan Didion was preparing dinner on December 30, 2003, when her husband suddenly had a heart attack and died. She captured the intensity of this heart stab in her book, *The Year of Magical Thinking.* Its opening words echo Hannah's prayer, "Life changes in the instant. You sit down to dinner and life as you know it ends."[1]

Isaiah 40, one of the *haftarot* for the Three Weeks, is filled with prophecies of *nehama,* of comfort: consolation after destruction, another reversal of fortune. Historically, it is "spoken" to the Judean exiles in Babylon who arrived in 597 and 586 BCE, and to the disconsolate Jerusalem after the siege. The Jews were told that their punishment was now over. It was time to return to their homeland and rebuild Jerusalem.

The words are a salve for the pain of alienation and destruction. The *haftara* continues in rising expectations and comfort as we move from tenderness and reconciliation to joy and homecoming: "A voice rings out: 'Clear in the desert a road for the Lord! Level in the wilderness a highway for our God! Let every valley be raised…'" (Isaiah 40:3–4).

The last verses of the *haftara* celebrate the power of God to change the fortunes of human beings: those who are powerful are laid low while those who are suffering rejoice. Through gentle poetic language, Isaiah rebuilds the relationship of the exile to his homeland, and God to His children. The story of exile and redemption is hardly new – it is stamped all over the Hebrew Bible.

It is so much the story of our people that a medieval rabbi believed the *haftara* to actually be referring to the exile of his own day. Rabbi Abraham Ibn Ezra, the great Jewish poet and commentator who died in 1167,[2] did not live in a time of national exile but in personal exile. In 1140, he was banished from Muslim Spain in unclear circumstances and went to Italy. Life changed dramatically for him; gone were the philosophers and garden poets of Muslim Spain. This great literary figure began

---

1. Joan Didion, *The Year of Magical Thinking* (New York: Vintage, 2007), p. 3.
2. This date of death is given by Nahum Sarna in "Abraham Ibn Ezra as an Exegete" in *Rabbi Abraham Ibn Ezra: Studies in the Writings of a Twelfth-Century Jewish Polymath,* eds. Isadore Twersky and Jay M. Harris (Cambridge, MA: Harvard University Press, 1993), pp. 1–27.

to write biblical commentary because he was sensitive to his surroundings. Christian Italy would not appreciate his poetry. He also believed that he was not one to experience fortune in this life. In one of his short poems he writes that if he were a shroud seller, no one would die, and were he to sell lamps, the sun would never set. But his loss is our gain, as we dip into the pages of his rich biblical commentaries. Ibn Ezra felt the lonely price of exile and perhaps thought that Isaiah was speaking directly to him.

In actual fact, there was a historical reality that generated Isaiah's words. In 538 BCE, Cyrus, the king of the Medes, captured Babylon and sent the Jews back to the land of Israel. He restored his new subjects to their rightful home and is regarded in the Bible (Isaiah 45:1–2) as a savior: "Thus said the Lord to Cyrus, His anointed one – whose right hand He has grasped, treading down nations before him, ungirding the loins of kings, opening doors before him..."

Cyrus, God's "anointed one" – language used for kings and the Messiah – wrote a proclamation of freedom that can be found in the book of Ezra, both in Hebrew (1:2–4) and in Aramaic (6:3–5). The king did more than grant permission: Cyrus – according to Ezra – created conditions that would generate the rebuilding of Zion.

> Thus said King Cyrus of Persia: The Lord God of Heaven has given me all the kingdoms of the earth and has charged me with building Him a House in Jerusalem, which is in Judah. Anyone of you of all his people – may his God be with him and let him go up to Jerusalem that is in Judah and build the House of the Lord.

Isaiah adds that rebuilding is not a task for a select few, but for any person willing to make the ascent to Jerusalem. He reminds us that these are also weeks when we must build new lives. Reversing fortune is not only about what God does to change our lives, but what *we* do to change them.

Kavana for the Day

Think of a reversal of fortune in your life and how you responded. What made the transformation noticeable? Did it conjure anger or gratitude? Were you able to put it within a spiritual framework?

Focusing outward, consider a reversal in someone else's life, a time of change that posed challenges. Check in and see how they have managed the transition. Engage in a conversation about change. Turn your thoughts about change into a poem or a prayer, in the way that Hannah found the words to place her experience within a larger framework. Life changes so quickly and so dramatically that we need to find the words to capture the moment and feel the transformation.

Day Sixteen: 3 Av

Personifying Tragedy

There is a fascinating point of comparison between *Eikha* and the kina, "*A'adeh Ad Ḥug Shamayim*" (the eighth *kina* in many collections): the way that personification is used to illustrate tragedy. In *Eikha*, Jerusalem bemoaning her exiles becomes a grieving mother crying over her lost children. The book opens with the image of a lone woman that sets a haunting tone for its continuation: "Alas – she sits in solitude. The city that was great with people has become like a widow." Initially we do not know who "she" is, but the fact that she sits alone communicates vulnerability and loss. The continuation introduces the city that has become a widow. Then we understand that Jerusalem is a woman, a lost woman.

Some of the most jarring images in *Eikha* take a female form – the forlorn daughter of Zion who has lost her splendor, the maidens ushered into captivity, the city as a harlot. Jerusalem becomes a nursing mother with no milk, and a crazed mother who consumes her babies.

By making Jerusalem into a ravaged woman, the city suddenly has feelings; it assumes an animate life; it bleeds and needs and weeps: "All that pass by clap their hands at you; they hiss and wag their head at the daughter of Jerusalem, saying, 'Is this the city that men call The perfection of beauty, The joy of the whole earth?'" (Lam. 2:15). The fall of a city is more than the destruction of bricks, mortar and the cityscape. It becomes the collapse of a nation's heart.

In the eighth *kina*, mentioned above, a reverse process occurs. Instead of a city becoming a person, a human voice likens itself to the expanse of nature, taking on elements of inanimate objects. Nature is used to wail about the destruction – "Would that I could soar to the sphere of heaven that I would make the heavens lament with me"; the amputation of a person's limbs is compared to a broken olive tree, spinning words that don't stop are likened to a wheel, constellations are distraught. In perhaps the most powerful image, "The sun and moon howl together and refuse to shine upon me, / I would shriek 'If only my words could be recorded.'" To express tragedy, personification is used to the opposite effect. The suffering of a lone individual is magnified exponentially by the enormity of nature and its impersonal relationship to humanity. The sun and moon cannot howl like a human in pain. Suffering cannot be recorded for posterity in the sands of time whose patterns continuously change. We all have moments of illusion when we scream for the whole world to stop and pay attention to our pain. But it does not stop. Unlike a city that becomes a person so that we feel its solitude, the first person singular in this *kina* longs for the consolation and commiseration of nature to no avail.

This construction in both forms of sacred literature – the biblical and the liturgical – offers us two ways to relate to tragedy in circumstances where words never suffice. Where words fail us, images sometimes help create the picture of loss. A destroyed Jerusalem as a mourning mother is an image we may all sadly recognize. We will never see a howling sun which refuses to shine, and yet the imaginative powers are drawn to highlight the absurdity of it. Destruction, too, has both these faces: the pitiful and the absurd. On these days when our national history speaks to us in its most melancholy voice, it asks us to stretch the imagination and make what is animate, still, and what is not living, weep.

Kavana for the Day

Give animate qualities to an inanimate building. Take the *Kotel* in Jerusalem and have it speak. What would it say to the people who come there to pray? What history has it seen and how has it understood it?

To what would it bear witness? Use your imagination to give feelings to the stones and crevices. In the voice of the prophets, write down what observations, what anguish and wisdom it would offer us today.

Day Seventeen: 4 Av

When Absence Is Presence

Since memory is so unreliable and yet so necessary for Jewish life, the sages of the Talmud codified practical memory triggers around Holidays and historical events. Perhaps the most seminal event for which we need a memory jog is the destruction of the *Mikdash*. Living without it for centuries, and without any real substitute for pilgrimage and sacrifice, necessitated an absolute change in both religious practice and religious mindset. It takes more than one day of fasting and Jeremiah's lamentations to recreate the universe of faith that was lost. In response to this dilemma, the rabbis instituted a number of practices as daily reminders that life is simply not the same without a central sanctuary to call our own.

The *Shulḥan Arukh* codifies these laws and places them together in a catalogue of loss:

> When the Temple was destroyed, the sages decreed that throughout the generations one was not to build an edifice completely plastered and finished like the buildings of royalty. Rather one should plaster and finish one's home and leave a cubit-by-cubit space without plaster opposite the threshold. If one were to

purchase a courtyard that is already completely plastered, the
courtyard may be left to remain in that state; one is not obligated
to remove its walls.[1]

If what we lost was a building and the activities that building housed,
then our own personal buildings are to be compromised in some way,
marked by the loss. It is not uncommon to see an unfinished wall space
of about eighteen by eighteen inches, above or opposite doorways in
the homes of religious Jews in Israel and, more rarely, in the Diaspora.
When we enter and exit that space, we take a moment to reflect on
another space in another time, a space that we no longer have and cannot even fully imagine.

But the laws not only reflect large structures, they impact upon
more intimate settings, from the interiors of our homes to our very person. The *Shulḥan Arukh* continues:

> Similarly, they [the sages] decreed that when one lays the table for
> a festive meal, one should leave one place setting empty, absent-
> ing the tableware that is usually placed there.
>
> When a woman wears her silver and gold jewelry, she
> should leave off one piece that she is normally accustomed [to
> wear] so that she does not don a complete set of jewels.
>
> When a groom takes a bride, ash should be placed on his
> forehead in the place he dons his phylacteries.
>
> All of these acts are to remember Jerusalem, as it says
> [Psalms 137:5]: "If I forget thee, O Jerusalem...if I do not keep
> Jerusalem in memory even at my happiest hour."[2]

We are asked to observe a ritual of emptiness at times of abundance.
When we are gathered for a Holiday meal and the wine flows and the
table is laden with the best cutlery and china, we leave out one place setting. There is no subtlety to the statement. Something is amiss. Women
accustomed to wearing a full set of jewelry bear the slight irritation of

1. *Shulḥan Arukh, Oraḥ Ḥayyim*, 560:1–2.
2. Ibid., 3–4.

leaving out a bit of finery. A handsome groom must mar his appearance on the most obvious and visible part of his face. His forehead becomes a canvas for a spot of ash, the dirty, charred remnants of a fire that cannot be ignored by him or any of the onlookers, even on this, the most joyous of occasions.

The list of grieving measures continues with the minimization of music post-Temple, and then – in a rather dramatic close – Rabbi Yosef Karo, author of the *Shulḥan Arukh*, boldly states: "It is prohibited for an individual to fill his mouth with laughter in this world." This is not an ordinary sacrifice or a slight smirch on a day of happiness; it may not even be emotionally feasible. The law demands that we dampen a condition of joy rather than a situation of happiness, so that behind the forehead, in the brain, our minds be inherently transformed by a loss that took place two millennia ago. This law is based on a statement made by Rabbi Yoḥanan in the Talmud:

> R. Yoḥanan said in the name of R. Shimon b. Yoḥai: It is forbidden to a man to fill his mouth with laughter in this world, because it says, "Then our mouth will be filled with laughter and our tongue with singing" [Psalms 126:2]. When will that be? At the time when, "They shall say among the nations, 'The Lord hath done great things with these.'"
>
> It was related of Reish Lakish that he never again filled his mouth with laughter in this world after he heard this saying from R. Yoḥanan, his teacher.[3]

Occasions which normally demand happiness, like weddings or the festival of Purim, cannot be experienced with total joy.

In the aggregate, these laws point to an absence which is a presence. We create a physical and emotional void to mimic a void that we do not know. It is more honest than filling in that void with memories we never experienced. Loss is not always about the fullness of memory but about its vast silences. We inherited the void, and sometimes we must

---

3. *Berakhot* 31a, Soncino edition, translated by Maurice Simon (London, Soncino Press, 1984).

occupy it by creating small reminders of loss through sensual absences – the visual reminder of a wall unplastered or a forehead marked, the tactile reminder of a ring not worn, or the auditory reminder of the music not played. These losses are no great sacrifice, just small irritations of a grief not imagined.

Kavana for the Day

Contemplate the loss of something precious to you, perhaps someone you love or a time or place which you cannot recapture. What have you done to create reminders of that loss? What cannot be filled in with photos and objects that you therefore express in other ways?

Leave a place setting empty or take off a piece of jewelry or an object that you normally wear for one day to honor the memory of tragedy in Jewish history. How did it feel? How conscious were you that something was missing? Were you able to make the abstract leap from the loss to the memory of tragedy?

Day Eighteen: 5 Av

Speak Tenderly
to Jerusalem

I n a well-known *haftara* from Isaiah 40, the prophet utters the
words that Handel turned to song: "Comfort, oh comfort My people ..."
(Isaiah 40:1). The verse continues with an instruction of what to say, but
first specifies how to say it. "Speak tenderly to Jerusalem and declare to
her that her time of service is over, that her iniquity is expiated." Harsh
words and harsher realities must be balanced by love. The expression
"dibru al lev Yerushalayim" – speak tenderly, or speak to the heart, of
Jerusalem – asks us to imagine a conversation between an incorporeal
being and a city.

   Tenderness is a difficult term to define. In the dictionary it is
described as soft, delicate, fragile, easily broken, thin, fine and slender.
After all the cruel or indifferent exchanges, a conversation of reconciliation begins with tenderness, the recognition that both parties are fragile
and can, at any moment, be broken. If Zion is a disconsolate woman, a
neglected orphan, a trampled maiden, then speak to her broken heart
and bring her solace. According to Rashi, tenderness means something
very specific: namely, that Jerusalem is no longer a servant to foreign

nations. Other commentators understand that Jerusalem's divine punishment finally ended. These commentaries stress an outcome rather than a process. Tenderness is not marked by how you say something but rather by the relief that you generate by what you say.

God tells Isaiah to speak tenderly. This is not a solution; it is a method. Tenderly, Isaiah tells his people that there *is* a path through the chaos: "A voice rings out: 'Clear in the desert a road for the Lord! Level in the wilderness a highway for our God!" (ibid. 40:3). The image Isaiah conjures is one of magical realism. It is realistic because the desert is a place of danger and unpredictability. It mirrors tragedy in its waste and desolation. Yet it is incongruous to imagine a road through the wilderness. Natural landscapes of windblown sand, rugged dunes and isolated mountains cannot sustain the man-made infrastructure of a road. But the message is unmistakable: there is a clearing through the pain.

Isaiah provides the antidote to Zion's suffering. He proclaims in loud bursts the beauty of Zion and the goodness of the world. In this *haftara*, read right after Tisha B'Av, the verses become shorter, punchier; the images are brighter and filled with light and love.

> Ascend a lofty mountain
> O herald of joy to Zion
> Raise your voice with power
> O herald of joy to Jerusalem. (Ibid. 40:9)

What consolation does the prophet muster that could stir hope in the shattered lives of those who lived through calamities? Isaiah does not promise instant improvement. One of the underlying motifs of the chapter is man's mortality – hardly a comforting theme: "All flesh is grass, all its goodness like flowers of the field. Grass withers, flowers fade…" (ibid. 40:6–7). How can man's mortality become a source of renewed strength?

Isaiah compares that which is fleeting with that which lasts forever: "Grass withers, flowers fade – but the word of our God is always fulfilled" (ibid. 40:7–8). The prophet asks mortal individuals to attach themselves to that which is enduring. Consolation begins when we start to value that which ultimately matters.

The first step of consolation is not a tangible solution. It is hope.

Before change, there is hope. Solutions are usually rational steps that signal progress. Hope is never rational. As Elie Wiesel once said, "Just as man cannot live without dreams, he cannot live without hope."[1] When we lose hope, we slam the door on God. We fail to believe that there is a redemptive power in the human condition. A lack of hope may be the single greatest affront to Judaism. Indeed, "The Hope" is the title of Israel's national anthem. It is the underlying theme song of Jewish history. Perhaps this explains Isaiah's mandate to speak tenderly to Jerusalem. It is not about a quiet voice or a compassionate touch. It is an order. Communicate hope. With a voice of tenderness, Isaiah lets us know that paths out of the wilderness do exist. Restore hope and redemption can begin.

Kavana for the Day

Isaiah understood that consolation takes many forms, but whatever form it takes, it must be generated after destruction. Pain needs a relief valve. Isaiah created relief through tenderness. There is an art to leaving a tender moment alone, in the words of a contemporary musician. What do you think this expression means? Contemplate a tender moment in your own life.

- What made it feel special?
- What made it feel hopeful?
- How can you recreate that moment?

---

1. From Elie Wiesel's Nobel Prize acceptance speech, as cited in Sarah Houghton, *Elie Wiesel: A Holocaust Survivor Cries Out for Peace* (Mankato, MN: Redbrick Learning, 2003), p. 42.

Day Nineteen: 6 Av

A Heart of Stone

One of the most beautiful expressions in *Eikha* is "Let us lift up our hearts with our hands to God in the heavens." (Lam. 3:41). When we visualize this verse, we can imagine pieces of a broken heart held high in our hands, a gift to God of our innermost feelings. "Look, God, see our pain. See these fragments, these emotional shards, pieces of our heart. We show them to You. Have pity and compassion upon us."

There is a Hasidic reading of this verse that offers us a different image. It aids us in constructing a positive way to handle human hardship. When we are in pain, personally or collectively, we may turn to others for guidance or cry to heaven for divine assistance, but we still have to struggle profoundly with how to manage with the pain and how to feel about it. Rabbi Soloveitchik once made a distinction between pain and suffering: Pain in the physical universe is what we experience when we get hurt. Suffering is an emotional, existential state that can exist long after the physical pain is gone. It can be wrenching, seem intractable. In the face of immense loss, we feel our smallness and vulnerability. Rabbi Naḥman of Bratslav, Hasidic rebbe and master story-teller, used the narrative form to give advice about this difficult human problem.

As a thinker, Rabbi Naḥman rejected despair and believed that

humanity needs to cling to faith, joy, melody, and movement, author-
ing the famous statement of optimism: *"Mitzva gedola lihiyot besimḥa
tamid* – It is a great mitzva to always be happy."* He believed that communication with a *tzaddik*, a righteous man, is critical for the soul, and
that every person yearns for God. With that spirit in mind, we turn to
one of his stories.

A TALE OF SUFFERING:[1]

A king once sent his son to distant places to study. When the son returned
home, he was well versed in all branches of wisdom. The king then told
his son to take a boulder the size of a millstone, and bring it up to the
palace attic. The son looked at the huge, heavy boulder and realized that
he would not be able to lift it. He felt very bad because he would not be
able to fulfill his father's request.

The king then explained his true intention to his son: "Did you
really think that I wanted you to carry this huge boulder? Even with all
your wisdom, you could not do it. My intention is that you take a hammer and break the boulder into small pieces. You will then be able to
bring it up into the attic."

Many Hasidic tales center around a king and his son. The king
obviously represents God, the ultimate King, imagined in human form,
and the son represents the children of Israel. The king is both the stern,
authoritative figure and the sympathetic father, playing on the tension
that exists when these two roles are embodied in one person, much
like our prayer *"Avinu Malkenu*, Our Father, Our King,"* beseeches God
through the prism of two different relationships melded into a difficult
whole.

In this story, the king, as is often the case, tasks his son with an
assignment that on the surface seems impossible. No one can shoulder
such a large rock and carry it up to an attic. The king is, in essence, test-
ing his son's ingenuity. How will the son interpret the task? Will he have
the originality of thought to find a way through, or will he give up in
hopelessness because a solution is not immediately apparent? Although
the prince has been sent to learn the world's wisdom, he must pass this

1.   *Ḥayyei Moharan* #441.

test that requires more than book knowledge in order to be worthy of becoming king. Indeed, in most such stories the king tests his children or his charges in order to check their worthiness, and to prepare the next generation for the tribulations of leadership.

The son in this study does not measure up. He could not see beyond the size of the boulder to find a way through the challenge that his father posed. The stone was too big and heavy. And the father understood at that moment that his son's wisdom was severely limited. Academic learning is not the only, or predominant, requisite for sitting on the throne. The prince lacked a creative problem-solving instinct; he saw only one dimension in the father's request, and that led to paralysis rather than innovation.

This story also has a wider application. Suffering is at the core of the human experience. Religions like Buddhism aim at helping people grow through suffering rather than shrinking in the face of it. Much of Hasidic thought, based as it is on an eternal sense of optimism, also aims at managing suffering by breaking it up into incremental pieces, each of which can be carried up to God – placed in the divine attic, so to speak. The way to manage suffering, the king wanted his son to know, is not to shoulder all of it at once, but rather to chisel away at it bit by bit, and only then lift it. That way it can be borne, and carried to a high place – given meaning and redeemed before God.

Rabbi Naḥman implies that God wants us to "lift up our hearts with our hands to God in the heavens." But our hearts may be like heavy stones, which we cannot possibly lift. What we then must do is take a hammer of words and break our hearts of stone. Then we can lift them up to God.

We have another biblical verse that has been interpreted in a similar way. In Jeremiah we read, "Is not My word like fire? says the Lord; and like a hammer that shatters a rock?" (Jeremiah 23:29). In one Talmudic interpretation, Jeremiah is saying that just as a hammer can shatter a rock, so too can the words of Torah combat the evil inclination, breaking it apart so that it has little power to rule over us.[2] This is a wonderful approach to managing temptation. Instead of looking at

2. *Kiddushin* 30b.

desire as a solid, immovable rock that obstructs our way, we need to view ourselves as the holders of a hammer, who can break the rock into manageable pieces that will then present little challenge.

So often in our lives we stand in front of a mountain of despair or temptation, before an immovable stone. At the bottom of such an incline, our capacity to scale the heights seems questionable. We can't move mountains. But we can wear down the mountain, piece by piece, day by day, crumbling the rock, lifting it high to God, asking for compassion, realizing that we are far stronger than we'll ever know.

Kavana for the Day

Recall a situation in the past that seemed beyond your ability to manage: it may be a family problem, an educational challenge or a professional struggle. Or perhaps there's a mountain in front of you at this very moment, or a stone too heavy to lift. Write down what made or makes it seem so overwhelming and frightening. Now list ten small ways that you can chisel into this rock, and some reasons why you should offer up to God each piece that you've broken off. Think how this will make a difference.

Tackle the first on your list. Don't leave it until tomorrow. You begin healing your suffering now. Believe that the King has faith in your creativity.

Day Twenty: 7 Av

To Question, That Is the Question

All growth comes through discomfort. Sometimes we find ourselves troubled by a nagging, nameless concern that feels like a pebble in our shoe. It doesn't cause great harm but irritates with each step until finally we must stop to remove it. Discomfort alerts us to the fact that something is wrong. When we face situations of moral ambiguity or emotional turbulence, we have to pay close attention to our discomfort: we often extract solutions and grow as human beings in understanding pain.

The *haftara* of *Parashat Masei* (Jeremiah 2:4–28, 3:4), read in this season, is filled with God's charges against the children of Israel: accusations of betrayal, neglect and idol worship. One of the main themes undergirding God's anger is that the people have abandoned the One who can help them, and turned to idols that are useless and can provide no sustenance. This theme appears in several guises throughout these chapters, offering a "pebble-in-the-shoe" way to signal growth through discomfort.

Jeremiah 2 is filled with rhetorical questions of rebuke directed to the children of Israel, opening with God's pained "What wrong did your fathers find in Me that they abandoned Me and went after delusion and were deluded?"(Jeremiah 2:5). This question may represent an honest introspective search on God's part to figure out what has gone wrong in His relationship with the Israelites. More likely, it is a question posed to sound reflective, but is really an accusation, laying on guilt. This reading is underscored by the later questions scattered throughout the chapter:

> "They never ask themselves, 'Where is the Lord, who brought us out of the land of Egypt?...'" (verse 6)

> "The priests never asked themselves, 'Where is the Lord?'" (verse 8)

> "Has any nation changed its gods even though they are non-gods?" (verse 11)

> "Is Israel a bondman? Is he a homeborn slave? Then why is he given over to plunder?" (verse 14)

> "What then is the good of your going to Egypt to drink the waters of the Nile?" (verse 18)

> "How can you say, 'I am not defiled...'?" (verse 23)

> "Where are those gods you made for yourself?" (verse 28)

This onslaught of questions presents an exhaustive flow. Alone, each could stimulate discussion. Grouped together – some appearing one right after the other – they are a barrage of criticism, serving as a meta-phorical kick in the stomach. Winded, the children of Israel make no reply; there is rarely a good answer to a rhetorical question, let alone multiple ones. The interrogation forces the Israelites into a mental corner from which they have no choice but to examine themselves. An answer to one question alone does not satisfy the Questioner.

The poet, William Wordsworth, portrays the confused state of one who is constantly questioned:

But for those obstinate questionings
Of sense and outward things,
Fallings from us, vanishings;
Blank misgivings of a Creature
Moving about in worlds not realized,
High instincts before which our mortal Nature
Did tremble like a guilty Thing surprised.[1]

Questions trap us. In our mortal, limited state, we are surprised and stunned to be caught. Continual questioning forces us to look inside.

Our text reminds us that this is a time of inner misgivings about commitments and our role in relationships. It is a time to review Jewish history and our enduring spiritual bonds to God. It is a time to question ourselves.

Kavana for the Day

What is the most important question you have right now? Write it down. Stare at the words. How are you going to answer that question? What is getting in the way of an answer?

---

1. William Wordsworth, "Ode, Intimations of Immortality from Recollections of Early Childhood – ix," in *The Poetical Works of William Wordsworth* (London: Edward Moxon, 1837), p. 343.

Day Twenty-One: 8 Av

Words on Fire

Nicholas Donin was a French apostate who lived in the thirteenth century. He left Judaism, was excommunicated by Rabbi Yeḥiel of Paris, and was later baptized as a Roman Catholic within the Franciscan order. In 1238, Donin wrote to Pope Gregory IX in Rome, condemning the Talmud on thirty-five counts. Subsequently, in 1240 the Pope ordered that the Talmud itself be put on trial for its negative comments about Jesus, gentiles and other subjects of perceived offense. The trial lasted for two years, after which the Talmud was found guilty. Twenty-four cartloads of Talmud volumes were burned, decimating Jewish scholarship in France. In those days, before the advent of the printing press, all books were hand-copied – an arduous task, which helps us understand the momentousness of this act of destruction. Every word lovingly written went up in smoke, effectively killing the act of study for thousands of teachers and students. In France, the people of the book had no books with which to explore the universe of rabbinic lore and law.

The trial had a ripple effect, and throughout the centuries after the first, devastating pyre was lit, the Talmud was similarly condemned in other countries throughout Europe. In Venice in 1553, the kabbalist Mattathias Delacrut wrote:

Our books are lost, the little that we had ... In Venice they burned more than a thousand complete books of the Talmud, and five hundred copies of the Alfasi [a medieval commentary on the Talmud from North Africa], and other books without end, new and old.[1]

Rabbi Meir of Rothenburg (the Maharam, c.1215–1293) was the scion of a rabbinic family and a student of Rabbi Yeḥiel. Upon witnessing the painful 1242 burnings, he wrote a *kina*, a poem of lament, called "*Sha'ali Serufa Be'esh.*" In it, Rabbi Meir personalizes the Talmud, speaking directly to it in undertones of sorrow:

Inquire, consumed in fire, after the well-being of your mourners, who so strongly desire to reside in your dwellings,
Who yearn for the earth of the land [Israel], and who are pained and shocked by the conflagration of your scrolls.
They walk in darkness, unillumined ... [2]

Rabbi Meir speaks to the Torah, sharing the reaction of scholars who have lost their way because its words have been set on fire. Some interpret the poem as follows:

"They walk in darkness": Metaphorically, the Jews are in darkness. They no longer have the resources to ascertain the halakhot because all the books have been burned. Take the Gemara away from the Jew, and he does not know what to do.[3]

Rabbi Meir describes what he personally witnessed: "All of your treasured possessions were gathered in the open square like an apostate town, and [how] the divine treasure was burned."[4] Volumes of Talmud

---

1. See the full description in *Printing the Talmud*, eds. Sharon Liberman Mintz and Gabriel M. Goldstein (New York: Yeshiva University Museum, 2005), p. 228.
2. *The Koren Mesorat Harav Kinot*, 2010, p. 590.
3. Ibid., p. 595.
4. Ibid., p. 590.

were confiscated by Dominicans and Franciscans and set on fire in in the city's center, in public view.

It may be hard for us to understand just what a travesty book burnings were because it is so easy for us to replace books today. But it is not only practical concerns that create the anguish. Clearly there is a philosophical animus behind book burning which led German literary critic Heinrich Heine (1797–1856) to conclude, "Where they *burn books*, they will ultimately also *burn people*."[5] Putting the Talmud on trial is one step closer to putting the Jew on trial.

On Tisha B'Av, we think also of another book burning, far more ancient and closer to the heart of the day. In chapter 36 of the book of Jeremiah, God commands the prophet to write a scroll describing the future exile and destruction of Jerusalem. In *Eikha Raba*, the Rabbis suggested that what Jeremiah wrote was actually the book of Lamentations.[6] He was in prison at the time and therefore contracted a scribe, Barukh son of Neria, to transcribe the words he dictated and to then read them publicly.

> Jeremiah instructed Barukh, "I am in hiding; I cannot go to the House of the Lord. But you go and read aloud the words of the Lord from the scroll which you wrote at my dictation, to all the people in the House of the Lord on a fast day…" (Jeremiah 36:5–6)

Barukh declaimed the words and the people became mightily afraid. The scroll was then read to King Jehoiakim of Judah and his court. They feared nothing in it, and the king took a scribe's knife, cut into the document, and then threw it into the fire. Words that should have shaped Jewish life were consigned to flames.

It is from this passage that the rabbis constructed a law, basing it on the verse, "And the word of the Lord came to Jeremiah after the king

---

5. Heinrich Heine, "Almansor," in *The Complete Poems of Heinrich Heine*, trans. H. Draper (Boston: Suhrkamp/Insel Publishers, 1982), p. 187. Written in reference to the burning of the Qur'an during the Spanish Inquisition.
6. See *Eikha Raba* Proem (*Petiḥta*) 28, 3:1.

had burnt the scroll and the words…" (ibid. 36:27). If we ever have the misfortune of seeing a Torah on fire, we are obligated to rend our garments twice in mourning, the first time for the scroll and the second time for the text. We mourn the physical loss of the parchment, and we mourn separately for the destruction of the actual words.

But as in this chapter, in every chapter of book burning in our history, it is the soul of the Torah that has the last word. God appears to Jeremiah after the burning of Lamentations, and tells him to write it again:

> So Jeremiah got another scroll and gave it to the scribe Barukh son of Neria. And at Jeremiah's dictation, he wrote in it the whole text of the scroll that King Jehoiakim of Judah had burned; and more of the like was added. (Ibid. 36:32)

More was added the second time, enhancing whatever was lost.

Ralph Waldo Emerson once noted that "every burned book… enlightens the world."[7] The burning of a book only makes it words blaze clearer and more dramatically in our imagination. They may burn our books, but our words will endure.

Kavana for the Day

One of the ways that we combat the book burnings of our past is with the purchase of books in our present. It is up to each of us to own a Jewish library, both for our own spiritual and intellectual growth, and to be a role model for our children, demonstrating what it means to live by the word. Rabbi Samson Raphael Hirsch, in the fifth letter in his book, *The Nineteen Letters*, says that "The very development of man's intellect itself depends on means of putting it to use: on communication through words."[8] So many of these words of wisdom are included in Jewish books, but sadly, there are many Jewish homes today without any Jewish books.

7. Ralph Waldo Emerson, *Compensation* [Essay III of *Collected Essays, First Series*, 1841], (Rockville, MD: Arc Manor, 2007), p. 37.
8. Samson Raphael Hirsch, *The Nineteen Letters*, Joseph Elias, trans. (Jerusalem: Feldheim Publishers, 1996), p. 75.

Redeem our past by buying a Jewish book for yourself and your family. Help your children begin a Jewish library of their own. It is a legacy of language and a gift to the soul.

Tisha B'Av: 9 Av

Beyond Words: A Closing Thought for Tisha B'Av

There are times when words are on fire, and there are times when pain is so great that there are no words. We hear a survivor tell us stories of the crematoria. A natural disaster takes thousands of lives. Genocide goes unstopped. An illness takes over a human life and reduces it to indignities. These experiences are described with words, but never fully captured by them: words are a betrayal. Silence, at such times, seems like the only authentic response to tragedy. The Kotzker Rebbe once said, "The whole world isn't worth uttering a sigh for."[1] The sigh is a non-word that signifies disgust or resignation or despair. Tisha B'Av is a day of sighs. By the end of the day, we have created a mountain of such sighs.

Many *kinot* actually incorporate the sound of the sigh with onomatopoeic flourish. In *Kina 32, "Etzbe'otai Shafelu,"* we read:

---

1. As seen in A.J. Heschel, *A Passion for Truth* (New York: Ferrar, Straus and Giroux, 1973), p. 226.

Wasted by sin, hands wretched in pain.
Oh! What has become of us?"[2]

"Oh! What has become of us!" is the refrain, the repetition of words
when words lose all meaning.

We experience this tension of language in *Kina 9, "Eikha Tifarti"*:

Rise! Knock! Scream! Be not silent!
Even pray in the voice of a ghost from the grave.
I have suffered so that I am almost mute...[3]

We move from the audible, powerful pounding on a door, screaming
to be let in, to the still, small voice of a ghost from the grave. Suffering
makes us mute; it moves us incrementally from a world of sound to a
world of silence.

We see this process in *Eikha* itself. In chapter 2, the distraught
Jeremiah says, "Arise, cry out in the night, at the beginning of the watches;
pour out your heart like water before the face of the Lord" (Lam. 2:19).
Our loudest yelling loses its potency and turns into the water of tears.
Our emotional range moves from anger to denial, stubborn rage to
impotence, critical debate to irrational jostling with God.

A friend who lost a child once told me that for nights on end she
would scream until her voice collapsed and with it, her soul became faint.
She would complete this exercise of pain in a puddle of tears. Listening to her suffering, I understood that she used her voice as a sacrifice
on the altar of the human condition. No amount of crying would bring
her son back, but if she lost her voice, she would somehow echo the
universe of loss she now occupied.

As a youth, Rabbi Soloveitchik once asked his father why so many
questions in the Talmud remain unanswered. His father explained to
him that God wishes to teach us a lesson that "not every event and happening can be comprehended by the limited mortal mind."[4] The Rav

---

2. *The Koren Mesorat HaRav Kinot*, 2010, p. 528.
3. Ibid., p. 260.
4. Rabbi Aaron Rakeffet-Rothkoff, *The Rav: The World of Rabbi Joseph B. Soloveitchik*,

internalized this lesson when he wrote: "With all his broken heart and unanswered questions, the mortal must yet exclaim, 'Who is like unto Thee, O Lord, among the mighty!'"[5]

As Tisha B'Av closes, we find ourselves worn down by the litany of sadness. We have spent a day reciting thousands of words that perhaps can best be summed up with a sigh and a cry and a pounding on the door, all the non-verbal acts that ask "why" more loudly than words. And then, if we are honest, we retreat into the silence, the collapse of the soul when the words have spent their course. In that silence we stand as if to hear the silence of embers floating in a Jerusalem morning the day after the Temple was reduced to ash, and we look again for God.

Vol. I (Jersey City, NJ: KTAV Publishing House, 1999), p. 171.
5. Ibid., p. 172.

Essay for the Tenth of Av

Redeeming the Ruins

How do we behave in exile, especially when we do not feel as though we are in exile? We turn to Jeremiah, the prophet who foretold of the first exile to Babylon, for advice. He preempted what the ancient Israelites may have thought was the appropriate religious response by writing a letter to his followers. The gloom and doom that we would naturally expect the prophet to suggest – and that fills page after page of his prophetic testimony – is curiously absent from his letter. Instead, he presents a formula that strikes us with its contemporary resonances.

In chapter 29, we read of the letter that Jeremiah wrote to a group of exiles in Babylon, which he dispatched from the land of Israel with Elasah, the man whom King Zedekiah sent to Babylon to see King Nebuchadnezzar. In addition to Elasah's diplomatic mission, he was also to present this letter as guidance for the small but growing community of exiles. The chapter begins with the letter's intended audience:

> This is the text of the letter which the prophet Jeremiah sent from Jerusalem to the priests, the prophets, the rest of the elders of the exile community, and to all the people whom Nebuchadnezzar has exiled from Jerusalem to Babylon … (Jeremiah 29:1)

The condition of exile changes personal and communal identity. You are in one place but your heart and mind are in another. To quote Rabbi Judah HaLevi, "I am in the west, but my heart is in the east." To be an exile is never to reconcile yourself with where you are, but to live in a persistent hope of where you want to be. In the book of Esther, Mordekhai is the only person introduced as an exile, as someone who knows that he is not where he should ultimately be at a time of immense assimilation. Imagine the immigrant who, when asked who he is, always mentions the place he comes from and not the place where he currently resides. He lives in perpetual dislocation.

Jeremiah, perhaps realizing the crippling impact of dislocation on the soul of a people, advised against this kind of thinking:

> This said the Lord of Hosts, the God of Israel, to the whole community which I exiled from Jerusalem to Babylon: Build houses and live in them, plant gardens and eat their fruit. Take wives and beget sons and daughters; and take wives for your sons, and give your daughters to husbands, that they may bear sons and daughters. Multiply there, do not decrease. And seek the welfare of the city to which I have exiled you and pray to the Lord in its behalf; for in its prosperity you shall prosper. (Ibid. 29:4–7)

In line after line, Jeremiah adds to his demands across generations, not only in the immediacy of the day but with the foreknowledge that exile can become more than a momentary condition but a way of life, for decades if not centuries.

Build houses, he tells them. Plant gardens. Seek the welfare of the city. Building a house is a statement of permanence. This is Jeremiah's starting point. Yet as he moves on, we, the readers, realize that building a house is perhaps the least permanent act on Jeremiah's list of recommendations for exile. After all, no matter where you are, you need some form of shelter even if, as an exile, you build something temporary in keeping with your desire to leave.

Jeremiah moves from building houses to planting gardens. The Malbim (1809–1879) observes that planting a garden implies a longer stay than building a house since the process of sowing and cultivation requires time. He cites a verse from Isaiah that seems to imply the exact opposite of Jeremiah's thinking:

> They shall not build for others to dwell in, or plant for others to enjoy. For the days of My people shall be as long as the days of a tree; My chosen ones shall outlive the work of their hands. They shall not toil to no purpose. They shall not bear children for terror. (Isaiah 65:22–23)

Whereas Isaiah does not want others to benefit from the planting of gardens, Jeremiah wants the gardeners to take advantage of what good can be found while on foreign soil; to invest in their lives.

In a midrash on the famous psalm, "By the Waters of Babylon" (Psalm 137), the rabbis of old say that the question "How can we sing a new song on strange land?" was not rhetorical, but literal. The Levites, in their desperation, cut off their thumbs so that they would not be able to play their instruments for the enemy King Nebuchadnezzar (see Rashi on *Kiddushin* 69a). They sat, instead, on the banks of the river and bemoaned their loss. But the midrash alludes to something darker: by cutting off their thumbs, they made themselves ritually unsuitable for serving God in the Temple precincts after their exile (see Leviticus 21:17). Signs of mourning that are permanent can show profound loss but may also reveal a lack of faith in the future.

We have met Jeremiah on many pages here, and might not expect him to offer us a positive prescription for exile. Yet he does. He tells us to become good people, raise good children and be good citizens, no matter where. He also offers us the belief that a stronger people will make a stronger nation when the exile is over and redemption is on the horizon.

Isaiah, too, offers his guidance on rebuilding:

> And they shall build the old wastes, they shall raise up the former desolations, and they shall renew the waste cities, the desolations of many generations. (Isaiah 61:4)

We are the people who rebuild ruins. And when, as the Talmud teaches, we get to heaven and God asks each of us, "Did you work for redemption?" we can each say, "Yes, I did" with a full heart.

Glossary of Hebrew and Aramaic Terms

Aggada: Non-legal rabbinic writings consisting of narrative embellishments on the Hebrew Bible, advice, general wisdom and homiletics.

Av: The fifth month of the Hebrew calendar.

Avelut: The period of mourning.

Bayit Sheni: The Second Temple, lit. "Second House."

Bein HaMitzarim: The Three Weeks, lit. "between the narrow straits," a term from the first chapter of Lamentations.

Beit HaMikdash: The ancient Temple in Jerusalem, lit. "House of Holiness."

Berakhot: Blessings. Also the name of the first tractate of the Talmud which contains chapters on the texts and laws of blessings.

Ḥazal: A Hebrew acronym for the sages of the Talmud, lit. "the sages of blessed memory."

Ḥurban: The Destruction, referring to the destruction of the Temples.

Eikha: The biblical book of Lamentations, attributed to the prophet Jeremiah.

Gemara: Rabbinic law and commentary on the Mishna, developed primarily in Babylonia from the second to sixth centuries.

Haftara: Portions of the Prophets read after the Torah reading on Shabbat mornings and on Holidays.

Ḥazon: Vision. Used here to refer to the Shabbat before Tisha B'Av, called the "Shabbat of foretelling" based on the first chapter of Isaiah, the *haftara* portion for that Shabbat.

Kina (pl. *Kinot*): The generic name of the prose-poetry read on the Ninth of Av, representing a collection of such pieces composed over centuries.

Kotel: The Western or Wailing Wall of Jerusalem, lit. wall.

Maḥzor: Holiday prayer-book, usually for the High Holy Days.

Makom: God, lit. place.

Midrash: Rabbinic homilies on the Torah written over a period of centuries. See Aggada.

Minḥa: The name of the afternoon prayer service, taken from the name of the afternoon sacrifice in the Temple.

Mishkan: The name of the portable Temple constructed at the end of the book of Exodus, carried by the Israelites throughout the wilderness years, and later situated at Shiloh.

Mishna: Brief passages of oral law committed to memory and transmitted orally that were compiled in the second century CE under Rabbi Judah HaNasi.

Petiḥta: The opening of a collection of midrash, generally referring to the commentary on the first verse of a Torah reading.

Shekhina: The Divine Presence.

Shiva: The seven days of mourning following a death and burial and marked by many customs and rituals.

Shiva Asar B'Tammuz: The seventeenth day of the Hebrew month of Tammuz, commemorated as a fast day and the beginning of the Three Week period.

Shulḥan Arukh: The sixteenth-century codification of Jewish law written by the scholar, Rabbi Joseph Karo.

Ta'anit: The generic term for a fast day. Also the name of a tractate of Talmud devoted to the laws of fasting, among other topics.

Tanakh: An acronym for the Hebrew Bible, constructed of *Torah*, *Nevi'im* and *Ketuvim* – the Five Books, the Prophets and the Writings.

Tanna: Generic name for a rabbinic sage of the first centuries CE who studied, produced and taught Mishna, brief passages of oral law.

Tefilla: The Hebrew word for prayer, from the word *"lehitpalel"* – to judge oneself.

Tikkun: A correction or repair.

Tosefta: A collection of oral law dated to the time of the Mishna but not included in the Mishna itself.

Tzimtzum: A mystical term for contraction of the self.

Talmud: The Mishna and the Gemara together constitute the Talmud – the foundational, encyclopedic work of rabbinic law – whose redaction took place in the fifth and sixth centuries.

Zakhor: The command to remember.

About the Author

Dr. Erica Brown is a writer and educator who lectures widely on subjects of Jewish interest. She is scholar-in-residence for the Jewish Federation of Greater Washington, DC, and a consultant to other Jewish organizations. Dr. Brown is the author of *Confronting Scandal, Spiritual Boredom,* and *Inspired Jewish Leadership* and co-author of *The Case for Jewish Peoplehood.* Her "Weekly Jewish Wisdom" column has appeared regularly in The Washington Post. She lives with her husband and four children in Silver Spring, MD. More at www.leadingwithmeaning.com.

The fonts used in this book are from the Arno family